THE GRESLEY PACIFICS

Part 1: 1922–1935

David & Charles Locomotive Monographs

General Editor:
O. S. NOCK, B.Sc., C.Eng., F.I.C.E., F.I.Mech.E.

Published titles
The Caledonian Dunalastairs, by O. S. Nock
The GWR Stars, Castles & Kings, Parts 1 and 2, by O. S. Nock
The LNWR Precursor Family, by O. S. Nock
The Midland Compounds, by O. S. Nock
The Stirling Singles of the Great Northern Railway, by Kenneth H. Leech and Maurice Boddy

In preparation
The Standard Gauge 4–4–0s of the GWR, by O. S. Nock

GREAT NORTHERN RAILWAY.

HEATING SURFACE		4-6-2 EXPRESS PASSENGER ENGINE	3 CYLINDERS 20" x 26"
TUBES	2715 SQ. FT.		DIA. OF LEADING WHEELS 3 FT. 2 IN.
FIRE BOX	215 „	3 CYLINDERS	„ „ COUPLED 6 „ 8 „
SUPERHEATER	525 „		„ „ TRAILING „ 3 „ 8 „
TOTAL	3455 „	DONCASTER 1922.	WEIGHT OF ENGINE 92 TONS 9 CWTS.
GRATE AREA	41.25 „		„ „ TENDER 56 „ 6 „
BOILER PRESSURE 180 LBS.			TOTAL 148 „ 15 „

Official photograph of 4—6—2 No 1470, signed by Gresley

DAVID & CHARLES LOCOMOTIVE MONOGRAPHS

THE GRESLEY PACIFICS

PART 1 : 1922–1935

O. S. NOCK, B.Sc., C.Eng., F.I.C.E., F.I.Mech.E.

DAVID & CHARLES : NEWTON ABBOT

0 7153 6336 0

Filmset in 10/11 pt Plantin
by Keyspools Ltd Golborne Lancs
and printed in Great Britain
by Clarke Doble & Brendon Limited, Plymouth
for David & Charles (Holdings) Limited
South Devon House Newton Abbot Devon

CONTENTS

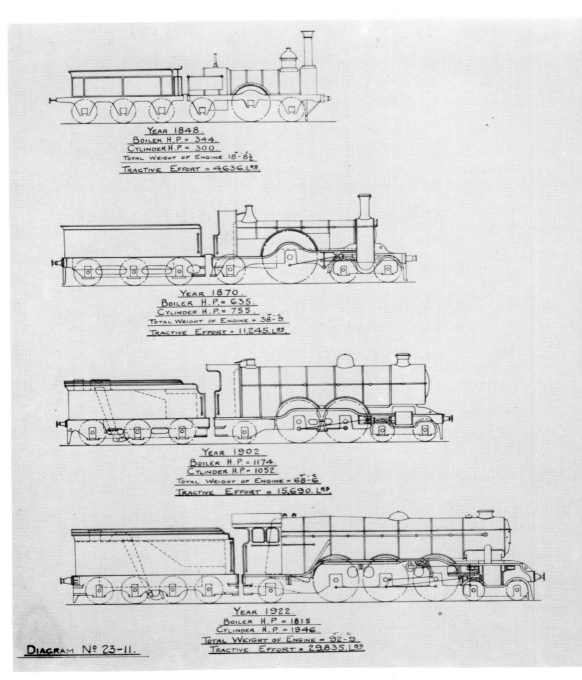

Year 1848.
Boiler H.P. = 344.
Cylinder H.P. = 300.
Total Weight of Engine 18-8½
Tractive Effort = 4636. Lbs

Year 1870.
Boiler H.P. = 635.
Cylinder H.P. = 755.
Total Weight of Engine = 38-9
Tractive Effort = 11,245. Lbs

Year 1902.
Boiler H.P. = 1174.
Cylinder H.P. = 1052.
Total Weight of Engine = 68-6
Tractive Effort = 15,690. Lbs

Year 1922.
Boiler H.P. = 1815.
Cylinder H.P. = 1946.
Total Weight of Engine = 92-9
Tractive Effort = 29,835. Lbs

Diagram No 23-11.

Development of GNR locomotive design, 1848–1922

PREFACE

THE Gresley Pacifics are always likely to remain one of the most favoured groups of locomotives in popular esteem. They provided the centre-piece of the very first book I ever wrote: *The Locomotives of Sir Nigel Gresley*, and when the original articles that formed the basis of that book were appearing serially in *The Railway Magazine*, it was a pleasure to me to know that Sir Nigel himself read the proof sheets of the earlier instalments, including most importantly that dealing with the first 'Pacifics', and their development up to the stage of long travel valves.

Many men of the LNER have given me invaluable help in the collection of data that is now incorporated in the present book. There is particularly the late Bert Spencer, who was so intimately connected with the entire development, and who had the experience of participating in the final developments in the constructional details of the engines, under K. J. Cook, as will be related in the second volume of this book. To the Running Superintendents, I. S. W. Groom, G. A. Musgrave, F. H. Petty, C. M. Stedman and E. D. Trask I am indebted for many foot-plate passes, while the friendship and help shown to me by various district officers, Spark at Kings Cross, Longley at Newcastle, and certainly not least Tom Matthewson-Dick who I first met at York shortly after the war, and

At the start of the Gresley regime: up stopping train near Hadley Wood hauled by Stirling 7 ft 6 in
2—2—2 rebuilt with Ivatt boiler: not scrapped till 1913

who has not long retired from the post of Assistant General Manager of the Western Region of British Railways.

In the early days, and indeed until some time after nationalisation, it was not usual on the LNER to put an inspector on when a visitor was riding on the footplate; but in later years, when I had the pleasure of meeting Messrs Black (Haymarket), Dixon (Kings Cross), Fisher (York), Harland (Kings Cross) and Stedman (Gateshead) they, as always with their fraternity, filled in many details on the practical side of 'Pacific' working. To all of them my thanks are due.

So far as day-to-day running is concerned, which is, after all, the end-product of any loco-motive design, I have referred freely to the files of *The Engineer, The Locomotive Magazine* and *The Railway Magazine*, and in the last mentioned particularly to contemporary instalments of the 'Locomotive Practice and Performance' feature

then conducted by the late Cecil J. Allen. But my most patent debt is to Mr E. G. Marsden, who as Information Agent of the LNER in the mid-1930s was instrumental in arranging many facilities for me to observe at first hand the working of the Gresley 'Pacifics'.

In recent years I have had the pleasure of meeting Mrs Violet Godfrey, daughter of Sir Nigel Gresley, and of hearing from her many reminiscences of her father. It is through her kindness that I am able to reproduce some of the more 'personal' illustrations in this book, including the frontispiece plate of the engine *Great Northern* autographed by her father.

O. S. NOCK

Silver Cedars
High Bannerdown,
Batheaston,
Bath
January 1973

Gresley in holiday mood, with King George VI, when Duke of York, on the Romney, Hythe and Dymchurch Railway

CHAPTER 1

THE FASCINATING PRELIMINARIES

THE locomotive history of the Great Northern Railway is a long catalogue of curious contradictions. In early days there was Archibald Sturrock, the man from Swindon, trained under Daniel Gooch, who was vying with McConnell of the North Western as to who could most thoroughly cast in their teeth the legend of pre-eminence fostered by the protagonists of the broad gauge. Mighty engines though both men built their influence was short. McConnell was too hot for the penny-wise management of the North Western to hold, and as a consequence he moved to Australia; Sturrock married into great wealth and forsook the rigours of Doncaster for the leisured ease of a country squire. And while the Great Northern abandoned his massive, superbly conceived '264' class 2—4—0 for the sleek, modest-boilered elegance of the Stirling 'straightbacks' it was the Northern Railway of France that adopted the Sturrock tradition, and developed the famous 'Outrance' 4—4—0 directly from the GNR '264'.

Stirling himself had his inconsistencies; while the great majority of his engines—passenger, goods and suburban tanks alike—had inside cylinders, and all the 'works' most discreetly hidden, his favourite engines were the legendary 8 ft bogie singles, with outside cylinders, and the great driving wheels almost indecently exposed! Ivatt changed all that, and went to such extremes in reversing Stirling's practice of big cylinders and small boilers, that his tremendously impressive '251' class 'Atlantics' of 1902 were so hamstrung at the front end that they could not use the vast quantities of steam generated in their huge boilers. The train schedules of the early 1900s were not demanding however, and when Ivatt turned to superheating, in 1910, he lowered the boiler pressure on the new 'Atlantics' so that with somewhat larger

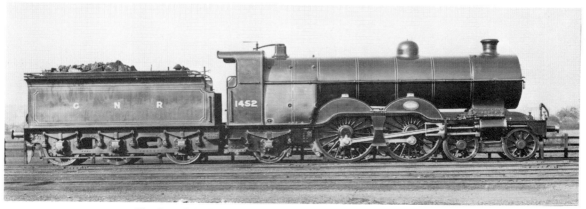

The first of the Ivatt superheater 'Atlantics', built Doncaster 1910

cylinders the tractive effort of the superheated 1452–1461 series was no greater than the earlier saturated engines. Then came Gresley, and it is significant of the lack of need for enhanced express passenger motive power that all new engines built at Doncaster in the first ten years of his chieftainship were for heavy freight, mixed traffic, or suburban passenger service.

His new designs nevertheless revealed trends that were new to Doncaster. By 1912 the 'Mogul' type was becoming popular for mixed traffic in Great Britain, but Gresley's was the first to have outside cylinders combined with outside Walschaerts valve gear; and the same basic engine layout was applied to his big 2—8—0 mineral engines. At the southern end of the GN main line, between Peterborough and Hornsey, Gresley had *in excelsis* the same kind of haulage problem that is prevalent in a marshalling yard: the constant starting and stopping of heavy trains. With the intermittent lengths of quadruple track, long running loops, and the necessity of giving priority to passenger trains on the double-tracked sections, the coal trains rarely got much of a run, and at many points the restart from stops had to be made on a rising 1 in 200 gradient. What his colleagues to west and north had done with their hump shunting engines, at Wath and Erimus, was certainly worth trying on the Great Northern 2—8—0 mineral engines—in other words three cylinders.

But Gresley was already becoming firmly wedded to the Walschaerts valve gear, while Robinson's 0—8—4 and Worsdell's 4—8—0 both had three sets of Stephenson's link motion. In 1915 two interesting events took place at Doncaster: firstly one of the standard Ivatt large-boilered Atlantics was rebuilt, with *four* cylinders and the Walschaerts valve gear; secondly Gresley took out a patent for conjugated valve gears for operating three sets of valves from two sets of gear. The 'Atlantic' rebuild, though not particularly successful, was interesting nevertheless, in regard to the present theme, on two grounds. It was Gresley's first attempt at combining the actuation of more than one piston valve from a single set of motion. The use of a simple rocker mechanism, as shown in the accompanying drawing, was not in any way novel; but it is interesting in the way it was contrived to have the valve spindles of the inside cylinders operating in a plane exactly parallel to those of the outside cylinders on a slope of 1 in $91\frac{1}{2}$, although the inside cylinders were much more steeply inclined. This matter of a difference of inclination of inside and outside cylinders was to form an important feature of future Gresley engine layouts.

The second point of interest about the design of the engine mechanism of the rebuilt 'Atlantic' No 279, was the single-bar crosshead used on the inside-cylinder connecting rod small end. As will be seen from the drawing, it would have been difficult to accommodate a lower slide bar in this instance. Though modified in detail the single-bar crosshead became standard on all future Gresley multi-cylinder locomotives, for both inside and outside cylinders. It is also interesting that in rebuilding the 'Atlantic' engine No 279 the piston stroke was increased from 24 to 26 in. The basic ingredients of a very successful locomotive would appear to have been present in this rebuild, and the lack of distinction in her actual work, and the cause of it can be no more than a matter of conjecture.

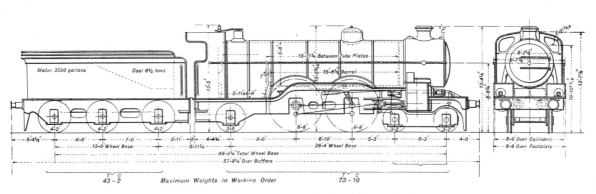

Diagram of 4—4—2 No 279, rebuilt with four cylinders

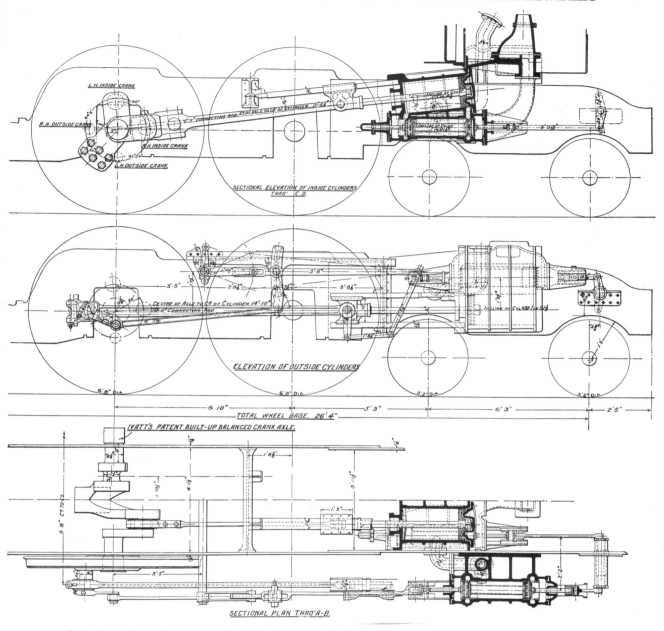

The 4-cylinder 'Atlantic' No 279: plan and cross-sectional views showing the arrangement of valves, cylinders and gear, also the single-bar crosshead for the inside cylinders

The steam passages look rather long and tortuous compared to the very direct and short passages of the standard 2-cylinder 'Atlantics'. Be that as it may, No 279 proved to be Gresley's one and only essay at a four-cylinder simple express locomotive, and the next multi-cylindered design on the GNR was another three years in coming. This time it was the logical counterpart of the Great Central and North Eastern humping engines, applied to the 2—8—0 main line mineral class, but incorporating one form of the conjugated valve gear that Gresley had patented in 1915.

In the adherence to basic principles Doncaster rather tied itself in knots over this engine. To secure the advantages of even torque from

13

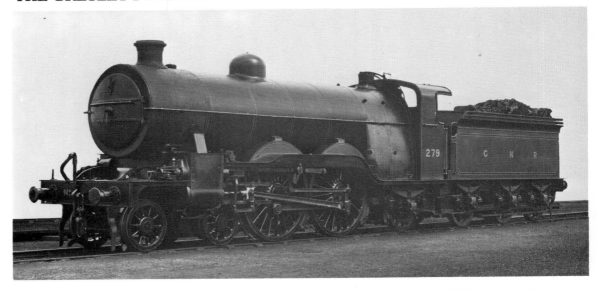

The 'Atlantic' 279, as rebuilt: then the most powerful express locomotive on the GNR with a tractive effort of 21,300 lb

the three-cylinder drive it was considered essential to have all three cylinders in line, and cranks exactly at 120° to each other. To clear the leading coupled axle the inside cylinder had to be steeply inclined, and so the outside cylinders were arranged likewise. The valves for the outside cylinders were placed above, and slightly inboard from the cylinders themselves, but the valve for the inside cylinder was a problem. It could not be placed in line with the others, because of the smokebox immediately above; neither could it be conveniently arranged beneath, as on the 'Atlantic' No 279. So it went in at the side, and the conjugated gear to operate it from the two outside motions took the more complicated form postulated in Gresley's original patent of 1915. Instead of horizontal levers the combining was effected by means of transverse rocking shafts, to which the valve spindles were connected through a multiplicity of cranks, links, and pin joints, as shown in the accompanying diagram. David Joy, striving to interest the Caledonian Railway in his very simple radial valve gear, was disgusted when Dugald Drummond fitted one of his '60' class 4—4—0s with the rival Bryce-Douglas gear, and called the result a 'birdcage'. With all respect to the Doncaster drawing office of 1917 the same *soubriquet* could be applied to the 3-cylinder 2—8—0 No 461.

The appearance of this engine, at the beginning of 1918 aroused much interest, and not a little criticism, in the complicated layout of the

valve gear, and from the purely incidental feature of the steeply-inclined outside cylinders. More constructive was the letter to the technical press from H. Holcroft, one of R. E. L. Maunsell's personal assistants on the SE & CR, but then seconded from Ashford to take charge of a Government railway depot at Purfleet. Holcroft pointed out that if a slight compromise were made in the spacing of the driving cranks, instead of placing them at exactly 120° to each

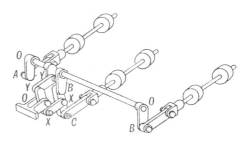

The conjugated valve gear fitted to 3-cylinder 2—8—0 engine No 461

other, the outside cylinders could be horizontal, and the simpler form of the conjugated gear specified in Gresley's original patent could be adopted. As a result of this correspondence, and of a paper Holcroft was invited to contribute to the Institution of Locomotive Engineers, Gresley called Holcroft into consultation over the design of valve gear for further 3-cylinder locomotives he was planning, and went so far

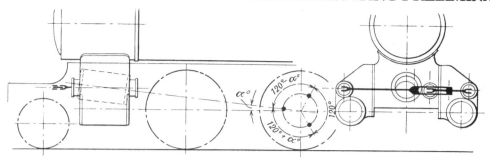

Holcroft's proposal for modified conjugated gear

as to invite him to join the staff of the GNR locomotive department. But the SE & CR were not prepared to release Holcroft, though the immediate and vital outcome of this brief collaboration was that the front-end design of Gresley 3-cylinder locomotives was firmly established on the principle shown in the accompanying diagram. If the centre-line of the inside cylinder was inclined to that of the outside cylinders by an angle α, the spacings of the cranks on the driving axle were made, successively, $120° + \alpha$; $120° - \alpha$, and an exact $120°$.

Thus if the angle of inclination was 1 in 8, or a fraction over $7°$, the spacing of the cranks would be 127, 113 and $120°$ and this gave rise to the slight inequality of the beats of a Gresley 3-cylinder engine.

The modified form of the Gresley gear suggested by Holcroft was first applied on the enlarged Mogul engines of 1920, which however, at that time, created more interest from their 6 ft diameter boilers than from the details of their valve gear. The criticism was sometimes

made of British locomotive engineers, and particularly of those of the old companies in pre-grouping days, that they were parochial in their outlook. This however could never have been said of Gresley, any more than it could have been of Bowen-Cooke and Churchward. In 1918 much interest had been created by the postulation, in the USA, of the merits of the 'limited cut-off' locomotive, and a huge freight engine of the 2—10—0 type had been built by the Pennsylvania, working on a maximum cut-off of 50 per cent. This was designed to prevent, positively, the uneconomic use of the locomotive by the driver, and the particular design proved so successful that no fewer than 475 of them were subsequently built, all *in two years* by the Baldwin Locomotive Company. Gresley considered that the more even turning moment exerted on the driving axle by the 3-cylinder drive justified a shorter cut-off than the British normal in full gear, and instead of the usual 75 per cent the new '1000' class Moguls were limited to 65 per cent. In consideration of this,

The second of the '1000' class 3-cylinder 2—6—0s

A contrast in boiler proportions: the first of the 3-cylinder 2—6—0s alongside the Stirling eight-footer No 1

the valve travel in full gear of $6\frac{3}{8}$ in was long for that period, and the piston valves, of 8 in diameter, were large in relation to the cylinder diameter of $18\frac{1}{2}$ in.

The new 'Moguls', of which ten were built in 1920, were intended for express goods service, but in the following year there was a prolonged coal strike which led to the cancellation of certain train services, the combination of some long-distance trains with others, and the conveyance of some very heavy loads. The ten 'Moguls' Nos 1000–1009, were all put on to passenger service and did very good work with trains of up to twenty coaches, between Kings Cross and Doncaster. It became evident that the new locomotives were very free-running. Speeds up to 75 mph became of daily occurrence, yet observations on the footplate showed that drivers were not handling them in the manner that became customary in later years with the Gresley 3-cylinder locomotives, but in the older traditional manner, with cut-off about 30 per cent and a partly opened regulator. On a typical run with the 10.51 am express from Doncaster, loaded to 605 tons behind the tender, engine No 1006 to Peterborough, and then No 1007 did excellent work. In summarising records of running with very heavy trains in that summer

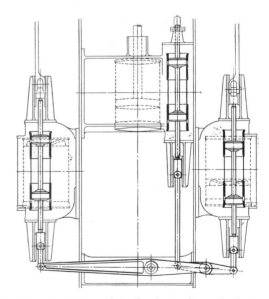

The standard layout of the Gresley conjugated valve gear

The 4-cylinder 'Atlantic' No 279 on a heavy down East Coast express near New Barnet

During the 1921 coal strike: 3-cylinder 2—6—0 No 1003 on combined 5.30 and 5.40 pm down expresses
passing New Southgate

of 1921, Mr Cecil J. Allen, writing in *The Railway Magazine* said: 'The "Moguls", of course, have all the advantage in starting and on the heavy grades, but the "Atlantics" show up as well and better on the long stretches run at high speed.' He then instanced an occasion on that same 10.51 am up from Doncaster in which the 'Atlantic' No 290 with a 600-ton train, ran from Huntingdon to Hitchin in only 35 sec more than a 'Mogul', No 1001, had taken with 440 tons; and he concluded the survey thus: 'But all these advantages should be combined in that long-promised Great Northern Railway "Pacific".'

3-cylinder progenitor Wilson Worsdell's 4—8—0 hump shunting tank engine of 1909

CHAPTER 2

'GREAT NORTHERN'

IN studying contemporary railway literature as the time approached for the 'Grouping' one is struck by the great disparity in the amount of attention given to the activities of the various railways. Much depended upon the reporting of enthusiastic correspondents, and, to take two examples, while almost every issue of *The Railway Magazine* contained a 'dispatch' from Crewe there was a deadly silence over locomotive affairs on the Great Northern Railway. The astonishing change that came over this situation during the ensuing decade is a measure of the interest created by the Gresley locomotives. The long-anticipated 'Pacific' was completed at Doncaster in April 1922, and by an enterprising feat of journalism, a photograph of her standing in Kings Cross station was published in *The Railway Magazine* for May of that year.

The official description, with all the basic dimensions came in the following month, but after that there was silence. Not until the October issue were there any photographs of the engine at work, and only then, for the first time, would readers of that journal who lived away from the Great Northern Railway main line have realised that there was a second engine of the class at work; and No. 1471, as such she was, then had no name. The pioneer engine, No 1470 *Great Northern*, was only the second Doncaster-built engine to be named—the first being the first Ivatt 'Atlantic', No 990 *Henry Oakley*.

Although there were some commentators who applied the terms 'mammoth', 'colossal' and such like to the *Great Northern*, she was in fact a very neat, compact, and handsomely

The first Gresley 'Pacific' No 1470 *Great Northern*, built Doncaster, April 1922

proportioned locomotive. How neat and well-proportioned the Gresley 'Pacifics' were was not perhaps fully appreciated until the ghastly rebuild of the *Great Northern* was perpetrated in 1944. That, however, is happily outside the scope of this book. Reverting to that momentous April of 1922 the general design of the new locomotive was generally as expected, and could be broadly described as a blend of the '1000' class Mogul, with its large boiler and very simple arrangement of the conjugated valve gear, and the latest development of the Ivatt 'Atlantics'. There was, of course, a vast difference in length, weight, and general proportions. By a coincidence the 'Atlantic' and the 'Mogul' were exactly the same length—34 ft 11 in from buffer to back of cab; the 'Pacific' was 9 ft longer, and 20 tons heavier. No simple 'rule of thumb' methods can be applied in settling the *structural* design of such a greatly enlarged locomotive, either in the framing or the suspension. I always remember a talk I had with a young draughtsman at Derby who was involved in the detailed design of the first Stanier 'Pacific' for the LMSR in 1933. He told me how they were greatly exercised to know 'how Mr Gresley got his "Pacifics" round curves'! Curves indeed; for while the East Coast main line, out in the open country is notably straight, there are some horribly sharp curves and turn-outs in Kings Cross station yard, and at 'Top Shed'—not to mention the main line platforms at Peterborough.

So, while the business dimensions of the new engine, cylinders, heating surface, grate area and so on, were of much interest, no less so were the details of the framing and suspension. It is no secret that these were not entirely satisfactory at the start. The drawings reproduced on pages 24 and 25 show the general arrangement of the locomotive. The frames were of $1\frac{1}{8}$ in steel plate, cross-braced at five places: at the buffer beams; the inside cylinder casting; between the driving, and rear pair of coupled wheels; beneath the forward end of the firebox, and at the drag-box. Doncaster succeeded in providing a degree of flexibility in the engine-chassis, by the use of frameplates $1\frac{1}{8}$ in thick. The most recent British 4—6—0s had $1\frac{1}{4}$ in thick frames. The suspension was a point of some difficulty at first. The GNR 'Atlantics' had independent helical springs under the driving axles, and laminated springs under the leading coupled wheels. The first 'Pacifics' were the same, and with laminated springs

under the rear pair of coupled wheels. On the other hand the North Eastern 3-cylinder 'Atlantics' of Class 'Z' had laminated springs under both coupled axles. F. H. Eggleshaw, at one time Assistant Works Manager at Doncaster, once showed me a photograph of engine No 1470 which Gresley had autographed for him, because, as the CME subtly expressed it: 'he knew that he (Eggleshaw) had been staying up at nights with it'!

The support for the trailing wheels was a novelty. The GNR 'Atlantics' had no side control on their trailing axle, and at times—as I had plenty of experience—the riding was disconcertingly wild. They were not *bad* riding engines in the generally accepted sense, and were in fact notably steady at the front end; but Gresley did a considerable amount of footplate riding himself, and was appreciative of a little cab comfort, and while maintaining the principle of flexibility in the framing felt that something better than the 'Atlantic' arrangement was desirable. The North Eastern 'Z' class had a simple bearing in the frame, but Gresley introduced the Cartazzi type of 'radial' slides shown in the accompanying drawing, providing for a side movement of $2\frac{1}{2}$ in. Although termed radial the actual movement in the slides were straight, though giving a good practical compromise for a true radial movement. The bogie originally fitted was of the 'swing link' type, as used on the GNR 'Atlantics' except that the links were considerably longer.

Coming now to the power-producing part of the locomotive, while the boiler had the largest heating surface of any yet put on to a British locomotive it was not the longest; for the distance between the tube plates was only 19 ft compared to the 22 ft 7 in of the GWR *The Great Bear*. When the full dimensions of *Great Northern* were known there was naturally much comparing of proportions of the two 'Pacifics', particularly as the North Eastern Railway published in advance the dimensions of the engine they had under construction at Darlington in the summer of 1922. It was clear that this latter was an enlarged, and much elongated version of the 'Z' class Atlantic. It is interesting to compare the basic boiler proportions of the three 'Pacifics', particularly as *The Great Bear* was primarily an exercise in boiler design by that master of the art, G. J. Churchward.

The Great Western engine had the usual moderate degree of superheat, whereas Gresley aimed much higher. Both *The Great Bear* and

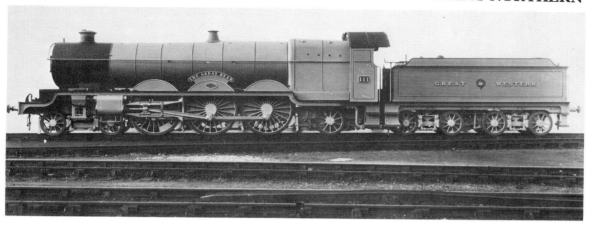

British Pacifics of 1922: Churchward's No 111 *The Great Bear* of 1908

British Pacifics of 1922: Gresley's No 1470 *Great Northern* of 1922

British Pacifics of 1922: Sir Vincent Raven's NER design; later example, No 2402 *City of York*

THE GRESLEY PACIFICS

Great Northern had the barrel tapered for part of their length, and on dimensions alone, having regard to the higher steam pressure used, the Great Western engine seemed to have the greater horsepower. In the latter the tubes were not so tightly packed, there being only 147 small tubes of $2\frac{1}{2}$ in diameter, against 168 of $2\frac{1}{4}$ in, and 14 superheater flues of $5\frac{1}{8}$ in against 32 of $5\frac{1}{4}$ in. The superheater on the GNR engine was of the Robinson type, though despite the outstanding success of the large boilered 'Atlantics' that Gresley had fitted with 32-element superheaters the heating surface of the superheaters on the 'Pacifics' was *less* than that of the 'Atlantics'— 525 against 568 sq ft.

Constructionally the new boiler was a splendid success. Its details may be studied from the various cross-sectional, and longitudinal views on pages 26 and 27. True to the traditions of Doncaster the outer casing of the firebox was round topped. The inner firebox was of copper, and all other plates in the boiler and firebox were of acid open hearth steel. In order to increase the firebox volume, and to allow shorter tubes to be used the firebox was extended into the boiler barrel to form a combustion chamber. While the shortening of the tubes resulted in a reduction of the evaporative heating surface such practice does tend to make a boiler more free in steaming. The steel wrapper plate of the firebox was in one piece, and was attached to the boiler barrel by a double-rivetted lap joint. The other joints in the construction of boiler and firebox may be studied from the drawings. In the form of the firebox can be seen the direct 'line of descent' from the Ivatt 'Atlantics', with the back part of the grate horizontal, and the front part sloping downwards. In this latter area a drop gate was provided. The boiler was supported at the front end on a cast steel saddle. At the middle it rested freely on a frame stay. The firebox foundation ring rested on a frame stay at the front end, and on supports at the back end, with shoes on part of the foundation ring to act as rubbing surfaces. The firebox was held down by a vertical plate which allowed freedom for expansion. The principal boiler and firebox dimensions are set out in the accompanying table.

The 'engine' layout was a direct development of that used on the '1000' class Moguls, so far as the disposition of cylinders, valves and valve gear was concerned. Coupled wheels were 6 ft 8 in diameter, as on the 'Atlantics', and cylinders 20 in diameter by 26 in stroke. As on the

'Moguls' the outside cylinders were horizontal, and the inside one inclined at an angle of 1 in 8 to the horizontal. It was surprising however that space could not be found for piston valves of a larger diameter than 8 in, which was the same as that of the 'Atlantics' and of the 'Moguls', both of which had an individual cylinder volume considerably less than that of the new 'Pacifics'. The volumes were, respectively, 5.66 (Atlantic), 5.15 (Mogul) and 6.02 cu ft. When one recalls that Churchward had been using 8 in diameter piston valves in conjunction with the 15 in diameter cylinders of the later 'Stars', and no less than 10 in on the $18\frac{1}{2}$ in cylinders of the 'Saints', it did seem that Gresley was injecting a restriction in the steam flow of his new engines. It was not as though Churchward was out of step. On the Great Central Robinson used 10 in valves on his superheater 'Atlantics'; so did R. W. Urie on the 'N 15' 4—6—0s on the London and South Western, while Bowen-Cooke had used 8 in valves on the $15\frac{3}{4}$ in diameter cylinders of the 'Claughton' class 4—6—0s.

Another curious point about the design was the layout of the valve gear. The 'Atlantics', although having relatively short travel valves were very free running, because of the very high temperature of the steam, their large, direct ports and passages, and a generous, if not excessive amount of, exhaust clearance. On the 'Moguls', largely at the prompting of Holcroft with his Great Western training, the valve travel in full gear was made longer, and the steam lap a little longer. But then trouble developed after a certain mileage had given rise to some slackness in the pin joints of the conjugated valve gear linkage. This, added to 'whip' arising from the inertia of the oscillating levers at high speed, produced over-run on the valve spindle of the middle cylinder. Two defects arose from this situation. The middle cylinder valve events went wrong, providing longer cut-offs than those obtaining in the outside cylinders resulting in the middle cylinder doing more than its fair share of the work; the valve spindle crosshead occasionally over-ran so much as to hit the steamchest cover.

These troubles on the 'Moguls' were very much in mind when the design of the 'Pacifics' was in hand at Doncaster, and Gresley consulted Professor W. E. Dalby, at the City and Guilds (Engineering) College, who was then acknowledged as the leading authority in the country on valve gear design. As one of his pupils I must admit that Dalby's approach to valve gears

PACIFIC ENGINE BOILERS

Railway Engine No	GWR 111	GNR 1470	NER 2400
Heating surface sq ft			
Tubes	2596.7	2715.0	2164.7
Firebox	158.51	215.0	200.0
Superheater	398.52	525.0	509.9
Total	3154.0	3455.0	2874.6
Grate Area sq ft	41.8	41.25	41.5
Boiler pressure psi	225.0	180.0	200.0
Length between tube plates ft in	22–7	19–0	21–0

DIMENSIONS OF BOILER AND FIREBOX

GRATE—	Length	5 ft $10\frac{15}{16}$ in
	Width	6 ft $11\frac{3}{4}$ in
	Grate Area	41.25 sq ft
FIREBOX	Height of crown } Front	6 ft $8\frac{13}{16}$ in
	above foundation ring } Back	6 ft $0\frac{5}{16}$ in
	Interior, length at top	7 ft $11\frac{3}{4}$ in
	,, width at boiler centre	5 ft $4\frac{1}{2}$ in
	Thickness of copper } sides & back	$\frac{9}{16}$ in
	plate } tubeplate	$\frac{9}{16}$ in and 1 in
BOILER	Outside length firebox, overall	9 ft $5\frac{1}{2}$ in
	,, ,, ,, at bottom	6 ft 8 in
	,, width ,, ,,	7 ft 9 in
	Diameter of barrel (maximum)	6 ft 5 in
	Length of barrel	19 ft 0 in
	Thickness of barrel plates	$\frac{5}{8}$ in and $\frac{11}{16}$ in
	,, ,, wrapper plates	$\frac{9}{16}$ in
	Outside diameter of smokebox	6 ft 0 in
	,, length of smokebox	5 ft 11 in
TUBES (small)	Material	Steel
	Number	168
	Diameter outside	$2\frac{1}{4}$ in
	Thickness	0.128 in
TUBES (superheater flue)	Number	32
	Diameter outside	$5\frac{1}{4}$ in
	Thickness	$\frac{5}{32}$ in
	Length between tubeplates	19 ft 0 in
HEATING SURFACE	Firebox	215 sq ft
	Small tubes	1880 sq ft
	Large ,,	835 sq ft
	Total evaporative	2930 sq ft
Superheater (32 element)	Heating surface	525 sq ft
WORKING PRESSURE		180 lb per sq in
Boiler Horsepower		1815

MOTION DETAILS

Diameter of piston valves	8 in
Maximum travel of valves	$4\frac{9}{16}$ in
Steam Lap	$1\frac{1}{4}$ in
Exhaust Lap	$-\frac{1}{4}$ in
Cut-off in full gear	65 per cent
Cylinder horsepower	1946
Tractive effort at 85 per cent boiler pressure	29,835 lb

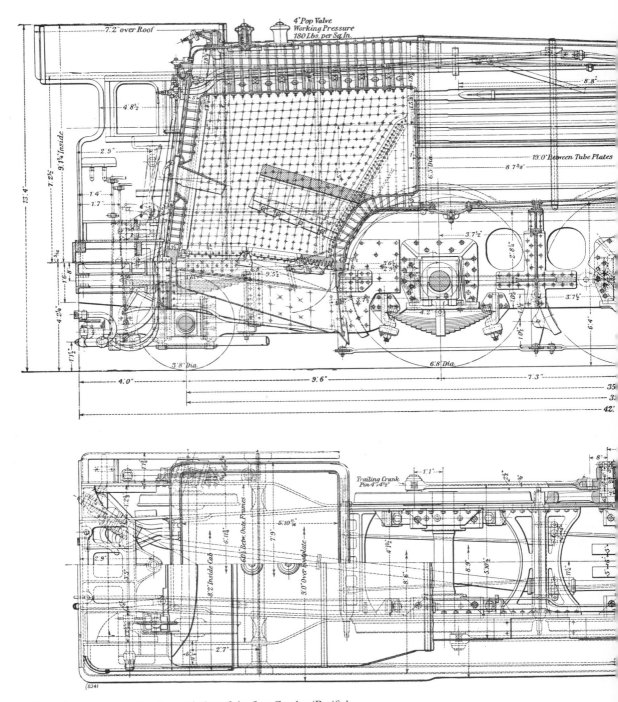

General arrangement, elevation and plan of the first Gresley 'Pacific'

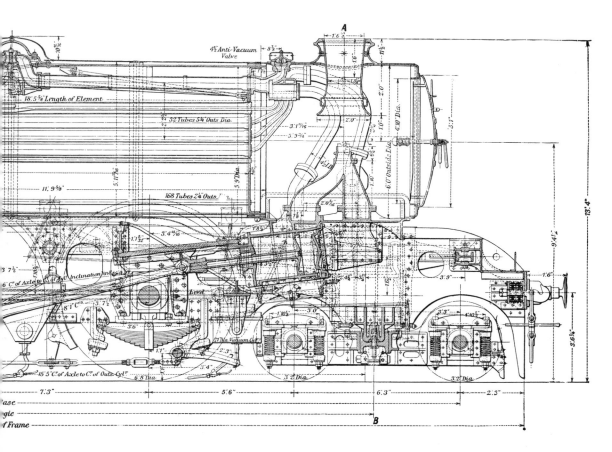

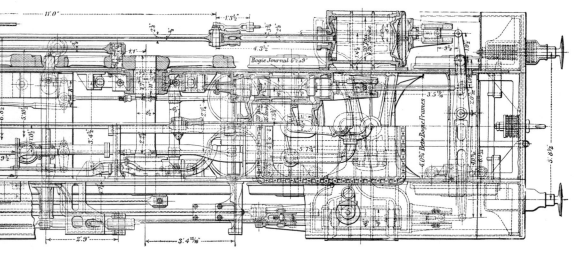

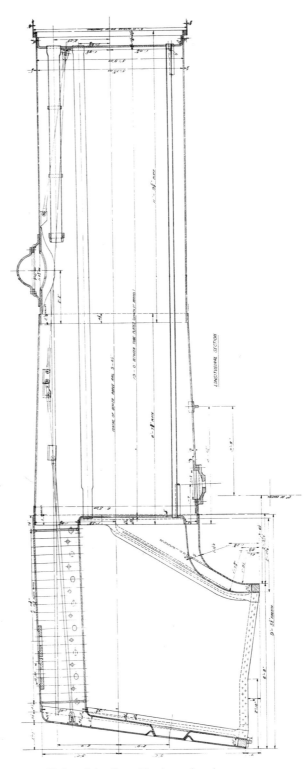

Boiler of the *Great Northern*, elevation

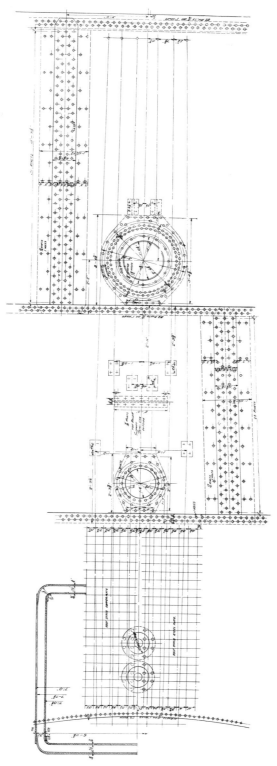

Boiler of the *Great Northern*, plan

THE GRESLEY PACIFICS

generally was highly theoretical, and in his various published works there is little reference to the vital business of providing for the freest possible flow of steam into and out of the cylinders. Whether the outcome of that consultation was due direct to Dalby's advice, or whether Gresley accepted the suggestion as a simple and seemingly inevitable way out it is not possible to say; but in fact the 'Mogul' layout was taken much as it was, and cut-off in full gear limited to 65 per cent. At that setting the maximum travel in full gear was $4\frac{9}{16}$ in, with steam lap of $1\frac{1}{4}$ in, and $\frac{1}{4}$ in exhaust clearance. It has been inferred by some commentators that the engines were inherently hamstrung on that account. But just as long-lap, long-travel valves do not in themselves guarantee a free running engine neither do valves with maximum travel of $4\frac{1}{2}$ in, and a lap of $1\frac{1}{4}$ in or less necessarily

make a sluggard. After all the Great Western 'City' class 4—4—0s had only $4\frac{5}{8}$ in travel in full gear, and $1\frac{1}{8}$ in lap. Nevertheless I seem to be finding faults with the original Gresley 'Pacific' design before quoting any of its earliest running performances. Such criticism is however made with the hindsight of what happened afterwards.

They were designed at a time when railway engineers were becoming increasingly conscious of the interaction of locomotives and track, and the old 'rule of thumb' ideas about balancing and its effect upon the loads transmitted to the track were tumbling. Locomotive men, anxious to put larger and heavier machines into service were pressing the argument of 'dynamic augment', or the effect of hammer blow. Bowen-Cooke had postulated the principle when preparing the design of the 'Claughtons' at Crewe in 1911, but got nowhere with the civil

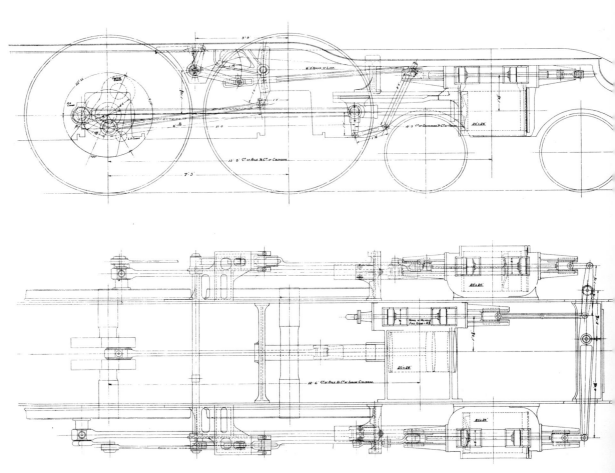

Layout of valve gear on the *Great Northern*

28

Elevation of tender of the *Great Northern*

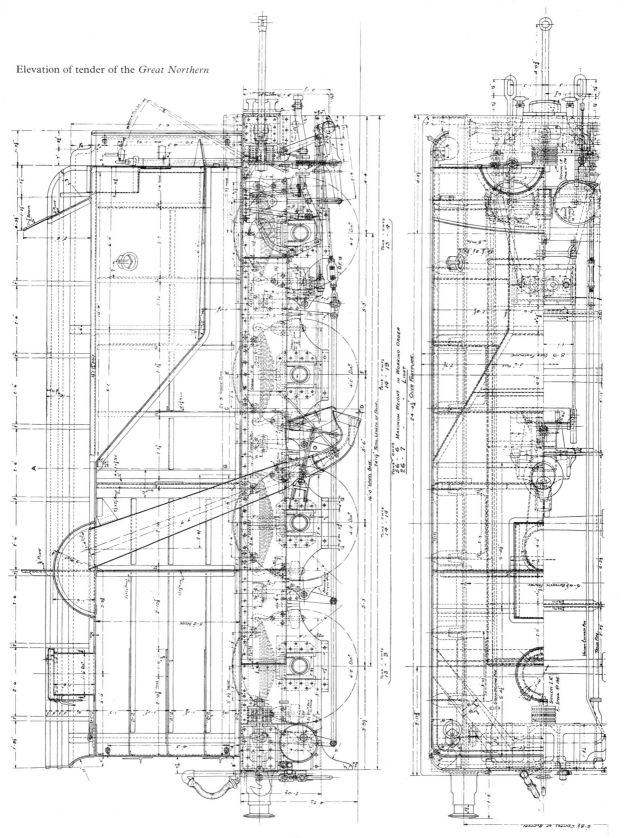

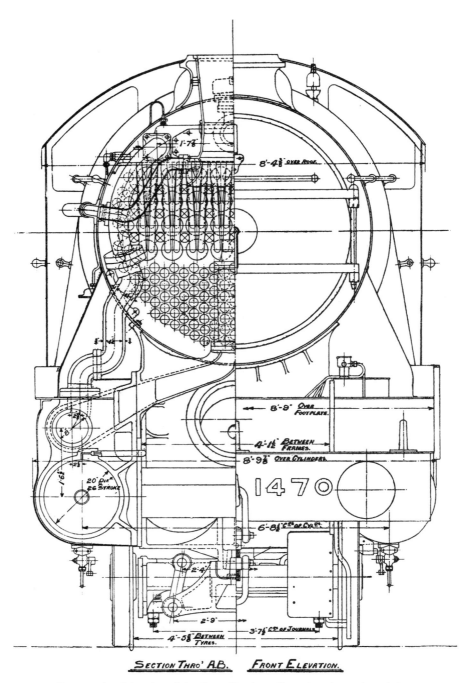

Cross sectional drawing of the *Great Northern*: front elevation and smokebox

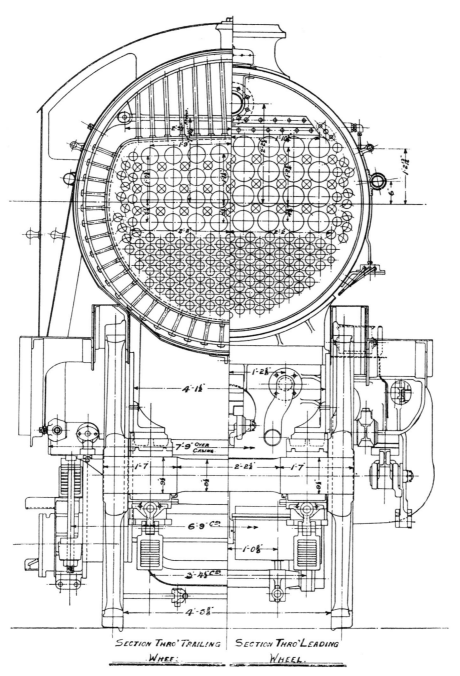

Cross sectional drawing of the *Great Northern*

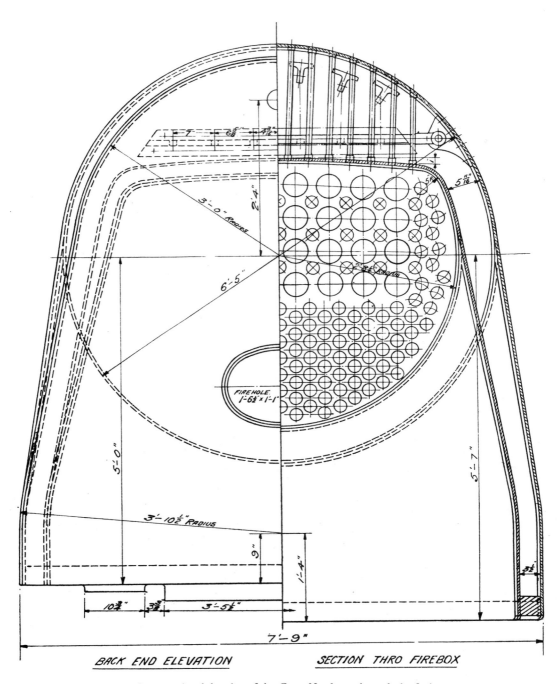

Cross sectional drawing of the *Great Northern*: through the firebox

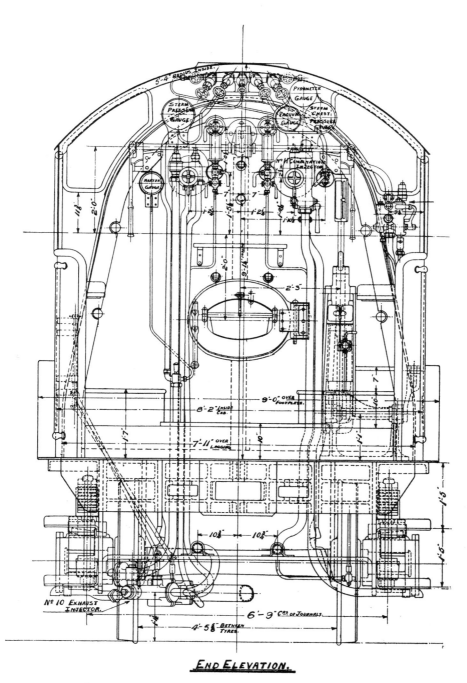

END ELEVATION.

Cross sectional drawing of the *Great Northern*: view at cab end

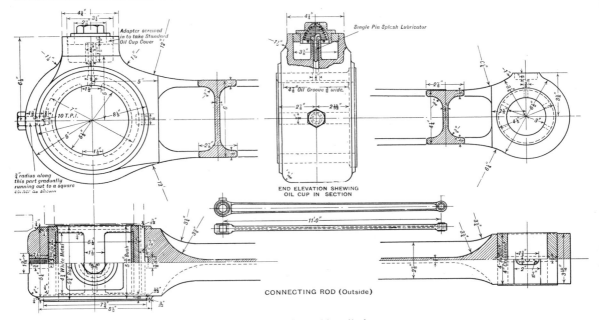

Connecting rod, outside cylinders

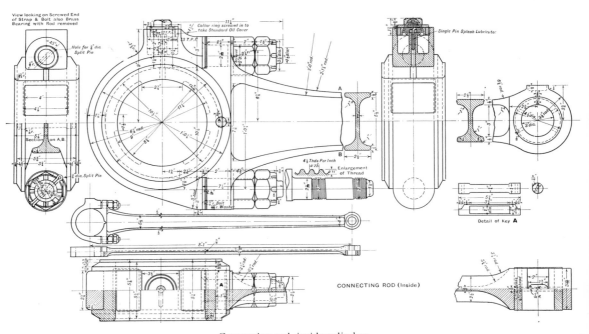

Connecting rod, inside cylinders

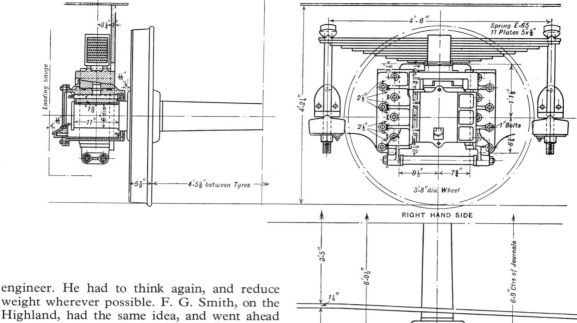

The 'Cartazzi' trailing-wheel axlebox

engineer. He had to think again, and reduce weight wherever possible. F. G. Smith, on the Highland, had the same idea, and went ahead regardless with the design of the 'Rivers'. The outcome there is well known! Gresley not only started with the advantage of three-cylinder propulsion, and the natural balance resulting, but reduced to a minimum the actual hardware of balance weights in the wheels by constructing the connecting rods, coupling rods, and all the valve gear members out of high tensile nickel-chrome steel, with a tensile strength some 80 per cent greater than ordinary mild steel. It was thus possible to make the rods much lighter than had been hitherto customary in Great Britain. This gave rise to some ill-informed criticism that the rods looked 'tinny', and that the design had been 'skimped'.

By one means or another the maximum axle load was kept down to 20 tons, though if an article in the July 1922 issue of *The Railway Magazine* was to be believed there were some startling variations. There the leading coupled axle was given as carrying no less than 24 tons, while the three coupled axles of *The Great Bear* each had no more than 18 tons on them! The latter was, of course, the weight with no water in the boiler. The official figure for the original Gresley 'Pacific' was a level 20 tons on each of the three coupled axles. With the handsomely proportioned eight-wheeled tender the complete locomotive in working order turned the scale at 148¾ tons, 6 tons heavier than *The Great Bear*.

The commodious side-windowed cab, was

something entirely new on the GNR, where footplate travel had hitherto been some of the most spartan to be endured on any British main line locomotives of the day. The new engine represented one of the first steps towards real cab comfort, with padded seats for both driver and fireman, allowing the former to do all his work while seated. Furthermore, the smooth-riding made sitting down the natural posture. I have ridden on many classes of locomotive on which evident care has been taken to provide for the comfort of the men, but which included such vibration in their going as to make sitting sheer purgatory. Standing one could absorb the vibration in one's legs. But on the Gresley 'Pacifics' one always sat. The controls were conveniently arranged; but not all of them were easy to adjust. The regulator valve was of the Lockyer double-beat type. This was a North Eastern speciality designed by N. Lockyer, Works Manager at Stooperdale, Darlington, and there it was always reputed to afford an almost 'finger-tip' control. This was anything

THE GRESLEY PACIFICS

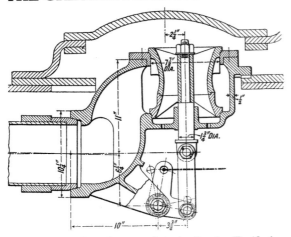

The 'Lockyer' regulator, used on the Gresley 'Pacifics'

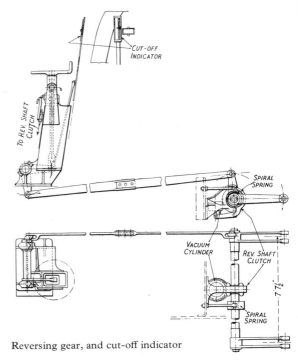

Reversing gear, and cut-off indicator

but the case on the Gresley 'Pacifics'. It always needed mighty tugs at that pull-out dependant handle to get the valve open. The vertical-pedestal reversing gear adjustment sometimes worked very stiffly too. On occasions when running inspectors invited me to take over the controls I always found a fair amount of physical effort was needed to make adjustments.

Taken all in all, the first Gresley 'Pacifics' had a wide welcome from all sections of the engineering profession and from the public interested in locomotives. The seal on this popular acclaim was very promptly set by Bassett-Lowke's, who had a fine $2\frac{1}{2}$ in gauge live-steam model of the engine on the market by midsummer of 1922!

Piston, as used on the original Gresley 'Pacifics'

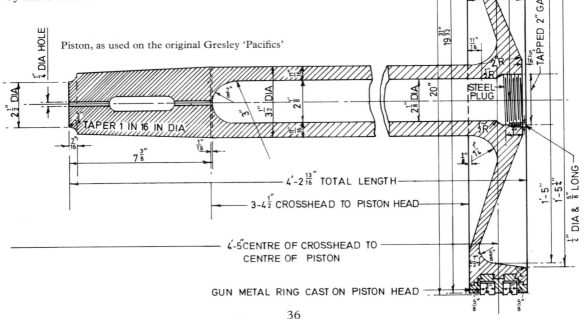

CHAPTER 3

EARLY PERFORMANCES AND TESTS

IN the autumn of 1922 one of my first weekend excursions after I had returned to London from the long University vacation was to the lineside of the GNR to see the new 'Pacifics' at work. I cycled to Oakleigh Park, and found a good viewpoint on the open-lattice footbridge just south of the station. Soon after 10 o'clock the 9.50 am relief 'Scotsman' came peppering its way up the long bank with a superheater 'Atlantic' obviously in top form; and then ambling along ten minutes after came No 1471, with the '10 am'. It was not officially known as the Flying Scotsman in those days, and it

certainly did not 'fly' either! My first impression was of a great engine working very easily, and the exhaust, in contrast to that of the 9.50 engine, was drifting down under a brisk westerly wind, and incidentally ruined any chance of a reasonable photograph. The load was little more than 400 tons, and with over two hours in which to get to Grantham there was no need for the new engine to be exerted. She was then little more than two months old, having been completed at Doncaster in July 1922.

Roughly a month before my first sight of her

The second Gresley 'Pacific' No 1471 *Sir Frederick Banbury* on 1.30 pm Leeds express near Hadley Wood (tender lettered 'GNR')

however she had been put to a severe test. The 'Atlantics' had taken trains of 450 and 500 tons on the fastest bookings then in operation on the GNR, and Gresley had made it clear from the outset that his new 'Pacifics' were designed to haul 600-ton trains. On Sunday 3 September 1922, their ability to do this was duly demonstrated on a run from Kings Cross to Grantham. Certain details were released to the Press, and published in *The Railway Gazette* for 29 September 1922. A twenty-coach train was assembled, weighing 610 tons behind the tender. The GNR did not possess a dynamometer car, but the engine was indicated. At numerous intermediate places the passing times were taken to the nearest $\frac{1}{4}$ min and from these, tabulated herewith, I have worked out the point-to-point average speeds. The start was extremely vigorous with such a load; but it seems to have taken its toll, temporarily at any rate. I have seen on the footplate, how heavy pounding in the first minutes of a 'cold' start can cause havoc in the firebox, and I can well imagine that the slow running out to Wood Green and the somewhat laboured ascent to Potters Bar might well have been necessary, while 'repairs' were being made to a de-ranged firebed. Then, although no mention is made of it in the published report, there would seem to have been a fairly severe check in the neighbourhood of Stevenage.

From Hitchin onwards the performance was magnificent, with fine speed attained down the falling gradients, and a splendidly maintained pace over the almost level stretches from Biggleswade onwards, as evidenced by the average speed of 69 mph from the latter station onwards to Huntingdon. But by far the most impressive part of the run was that north of Peterborough,

where the speed averaged 46 mph throughout the 11.5 miles from Essendine to Stoke Box, where the average rate of ascent is 1 in 254. The drawbar horsepower involved would be about 1350, and the indicated horsepower, estimated, at about 1700. The boiler horsepower of these engines was quoted at 1815, so it seems that on this stretch No 1471 was going not far from 'all out'. Again, the running on the fast stretches north of Hitchin was very free; a locomotive that could haul a train of 610 tons at 70 mph or so on virtually level track was certainly in advance of any class then in service in Great Britain. The report in *The Railway Gazette*, which clearly bears the stamp of Charles S. Lake's authorship, concluded thus:

It must be perfectly obvious to everyone who follows such matters that in these new 'Pacific' type express locomotives the Great Northern Railway have at their disposal a class of engine which, with train loads as high as 500 or even 550 tons, should be able, if it were considered desirable, to make non-stop runs between London and Grantham on schedules of 1 hour 45 minutes, or 1 hour 50 minutes, without encroaching upon their reserve power, or, alternatively, of taking loads in excess thereof of the best of the pre-war timings without any question of assistant engines arising.

No details were published at the time of the extent to which No 1471 was opened out on the 610-ton test run, and without a dynamometer car it was not possible to relate the actual coal and water consumption to the work done. There can be little doubt however that the coal consumption was extremely heavy. Mr Gresley stated at the time of the published report that the average consumption of No 1471 during

The 610-ton test run, 3 September 1922: engine No 1471 near New Southgate

GNR KINGS CROSS—GRANTHAM Test Run, Sunday 9 September 1922 4—6—2 engine No 1471 20 coaches empty stock, 610 tons			
Dist miles		Time min	Av speed mph
0.0	KINGS CROSS	0	—
2.5	Finsbury Park	7½	—
5.0	Wood Green	11¾	34
12.7	Potters Bar	24	38
17.7	Hatfield	30	50
25.0	Knebworth	37½	58½
28.6	Stevenage	42½	43 ★
31.9	HITCHIN	46	56½
41.4	Biggleswade	53½	73½
44.1	Sandy	56	72
58.9	HUNTINGDON	69	68½
63.0	Abbots Ripton	74	49
69.4	Holme	79	76½
76.4	PETERBOROUGH	86	60
88.6	Essendine	101	49
92.2	Little Bytham	105½	48
97.1	Corby	112	45¼
100.1	*Stoke Box*	116	45
105.5	GRANTHAM	122	54

★ check near this point.

the month of September amounted to 49 lb per mile; but during that time she was stationed at Kings Cross, and working for the most part on easily timed trains, with loads rarely approaching 500 tons. The Leeds and Bradford expresses were then more sharply timed than the Anglo-Scottish services, which were still running to the minimum times laid down in the 'gentleman's' agreement between the East Coast and West Coast companies negotiated after the Race to the North of 1895. The day-to-day running of the two 'Pacifics', and the fine test performance of No 1471 established the design as satisfactory, and authority was given for the construction of ten more engines of the class, to be built at Doncaster Works. At the same time a difficulty in their use was being experienced at Kings Cross. The entire station layout was very cramped, with the locomotive yard tucked in between the track of No 13 platform and the line climbing up from the Metropolitan Railway tunnels. The turntable at the end of this confined area was the largest that could be accommodated between the two retaining walls, namely 50 ft and it could just take an 'Atlantic'. When they were first introduced the 'Pacifics' had to run out to Hornsey to be turned. The turntable at Kings Cross 'top shed' was also no larger than 50 ft.

The success of Nos 1470 and 1471, and the decision to build more of the class highlighted the awkward situation at Kings Cross, and the decision to install a 70 ft turntable became part of a general scheme of improvement, including the enlargement of the suburban part of the station, and the provision of a modern well-equipped locomotive yard, to enable 'Pacific' engines from Grantham and Doncaster sheds to be turned and serviced ready for their return

Engine 1470 repainted in LNER style, and numbered '1470 N' leaving Kings Cross on the 5.40 pm Leeds express

THE GRESLEY PACIFICS

Pacific No 1474, unnamed, on the turntable at Hornsey, before the improvements in Kings Cross Yard

workings in the shortest possible time. While this scheme of improvement was not undertaken solely for the benefit of the 'Pacific' engines their introduction brought rapidly to a head matters that had been brewing for some time. During the winter of 1922–3, when the two 'Pacifics' settled down to their regular work, the inconvenience of turning at Hornsey prevailed. Engine No 1471 was transferred to Doncaster to join 1470, and the two engines were rostered to the hardest turns then operated on the GNR:

1. The 10.51 am up Doncaster to Kings Cross, returning on the 4 pm down
2. The 12.52 pm up Doncaster to Kings Cross, returning on the 5.40 pm down

The two turns were complementary to each other, in that the up journey was by far the harder proposition in No 1 turn, while in No 2 the 5.40 pm down was immeasurably the harder. During that winter Mr Cecil J. Allen made a number of journeys on these trains, and early in 1923 he wrote enthusiastically of his experiences, even to the extent of saying 'Briefly, there is no doubt that the new Great Northern engines very distinctly mark the beginning of a new epoch in British standards of express locomotive design and work.' He even went to the extent of allowing his enthusiasm to break through his traditional impartiality by suggesting, in the same article, that '. . . at long last, a British type has appeared—granted, a much larger, heavier, and dimensionally more powerful engine—which will, I believe, give a

Great Western 4—6—0 points and a beating. A bold claim, indeed, but, from my observations, one that is justifiable'.

The fires of partisanship were being well and truly kindled, and not only in confrontation with the West of England. Before the year 1922 was out the North Eastern Railway had completed its first 'Pacific', and with both companies merged into the same group as from 1 January 1923, it was clear that a decision would soon be required as to which 'Pacific' design would be the future LNER standard. But during the last months of 1922 the GNR 'Pacifics' had the field to themselves on the East Coast Route, and some reference to their daily work must be made. The 10.51 am up from Doncaster, with a load of about 450 tons as far as Grantham, and 490 to 500 tons onwards to Kings Cross, had regular stops at Retford, Grantham and Peterborough, but on Wednesdays made an additional stop at Newark. The times were not difficult, except when the Newark stop was called, and then 38 min for the 33.1 miles from Retford to Grantham was impossible. The 29.1 miles from Grantham to Peterborough were allowed 33 min, and the final 76.4 miles up to Kings Cross 86 min. The 5.40 pm down, with a load never less than 475 tons was allowed 87 min to Peterborough, 37 min onward to Grantham, and 55 min for the 50.5 miles to Doncaster. The 'Pacifics' generally had no difficulty in keeping time.

The ascent from Peterborough to Stoke Box

Engine 4—6—2 No								1470			1471	
Load, tons E/F								447/475			496/525	
Dist miles								Actual m s		Speeds mph	Actual m s		Speeds mph
0.0	PETEROROUGH	.	.	.	.	.	.	0	00	—	0	00	—
3.1	Werrington Junc.							6	25	53	6	25	—
8.4	Tallington	.						12	05	60	12	10	59
12.2	Essendine	.						16	00	60	16	15	53
15.8	Little Bytham	.						19	45	55	20	25	49
20.7	Corby	.						25	35	49/52	27	15	40½/45
23.7	Stoke Box	.						29	35	46	31	45	36½
29.1	GRANTHAM	.	.	.	.	.	.	36	15	—	38	05	

Schedule time: 37 minutes

was always a severe test, but a fair one, for the engine was then fully warmed up for the work. I have set out in the accompanying table, two runs, when loads of 475 and 525 tons were being conveyed, and which make an interesting comparison over this section with the 610-ton test run of No 1471 in September 1922. On the run tabulated *Great Northern* did well, and Cecil J. Allen, recording a sustained speed of 50 mph for a full mile on 1 in 200, referred to it as a unique feat in his experience. The equivalent drawbar pull at this speed would have been about 4.3 tons; but I have figures before me to show that equally robust efforts had been made, at that speed not only by Great Western 'Stars' but also by the North Western 'Claughtons'. The true superiority of the Gresley 'Pacifics' was not to be developed for several years to come. In the comparative run in the table engine No 1471 lost a minute on schedule, and her time of 15½ min from Essendine to Stoke with 525 tons does not compare with her 15 min over the same distance with the 610-ton test train

The first of the newly-authorised batch of new engines was completed at Doncaster in February 1923, under London and North Eastern ownership. The new company was very quick off the mark in deciding its engine liveries. Locomotives of the Great Northern, North Eastern, North British and Great Central Railways painted in their pre-grouping liveries, but with the initials L & NER surmounting large numbers on the tender sides were paraded at York on 31 January, 1923 and at Marylebone on 22 February. On the following day the

One of the North Eastern rivals: the Raven Pacific No 2402 *City of York*

41

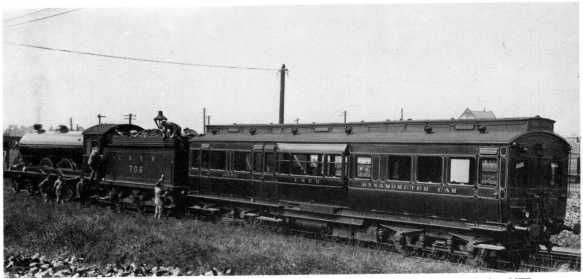

Dynamometer car of the former NER, used on tests of many Gresley locomotives, attached to NER 3-cylinder Atlantic No 706

decision was taken to paint express engines in the GNR shade of green, but without the red underframes, and without the dark green surround to the tender panel. For the record, the express locomotives displayed were GNR large 'Atlantic' No 1418; NER 'Z' class No 2169; NBR 4—4—2 No 874 *Dunedin*, and GCR 'Director' class 4—4—0 No 503 *Somme*. The first of the new GNR type 'Pacifics', No 1472, was turned out in the new painting style. The rest of the new batch came fairly slowly from Doncaster: Nos 1473 and 1474 in March; 1475 in April; 1476 in May; 1477 and 1478 in June; 1479 in July; and the remaining two in August.

In the meantime the all-important post of Chief Mechanical Engineer of the new group had been settled at the end of February. It is now well known that it was first offered to J. G. Robinson. With the retirement of Sir Vincent Raven the Great Central CME was by many years the senior, in office, of the locomotive chiefs of the constituent companies, and he had a distinguished record of service. He was however then more than sixty-seven years of age, and had been CME of the Great Central for twenty years. Although there was then no hard-and-fast age limit for the retirement of senior officers—and C. B. Collett on the GWR continued until he was seventy—Robinson felt that a younger man was needed, one who could not only steer through the initial period of co-ordination, after grouping, but who could continue to develop policy and design for some years thereafter. Putting this point of view to his former chairman, Lord Faringdon, and to the new chairman of the LNER, William Whitelaw, he had virtually nominated Gresley for the job. At the end of February 1923 Gresley was duly appointed.

With North Eastern resources added to those of the Great Northern, Gresley now had the Darlington dynamometer car and its experienced staff at his disposal, and at midsummer 1923 a series of trials was run between the first of the new Doncaster 'Pacifics', No 1472, and the first Raven Pacific, No 2400. For the purpose of these trials the engine workings from Doncaster shed were re-arranged so that the two hardest turns—10.51 am up and 5.40 pm down—could be worked by the same engine. Although it might possibly have seemed that the adoption of the Gresley design as the future LNER standard was a foregone conclusion the North Eastern entered into the competition—for such it certainly was—with the utmost determination. In charge of No 2400 was a superb engine crew, in Driver Tom Blades of Gateshead, and Fireman Charlie Fisher. Blades was fireman to the great Bob Nicholson on the 'M' class 4—4—0 engine No 1620 in the closing stages of the Race to the North in 1895; Fisher, in later years, became a locomotive running inspector at York and I had many footplate journeys with him. Between them they certainly upheld the honour of the North Eastern.

The results were conveyed to Gresley in a memorandum from the Darlington drawing office dated 21 July 1923, copies of which were made available to me some years later by Mr K. J. Cook, when he was chief mechanical and electrical engineer of the Eastern and North Eastern Regions of British Railways. Before referring in particular to the accompanying tables of test results, the description of methods used in making the test may be quoted, from the official report.

Method of Conducting Tests

Number of tests, and trains worked

Tests commenced June 25th. and terminated July 4th. tests being run on 9 days.

On June 26th. Engine 1472 could not work return trip owing to side rod bush hot on left driving crank pin.

On June 27th. Dynamometer Car drawbar hook was broken at Grantham on outward trip.

On June 30th. Engine 2400 could not work return trip owing to side rod bush hot on left driving crank pin.

The results shown on Sheet 1 are for the six days on which satisfactory runs were got in both directions.

With the exception of June 28th. on which the 12.52 p.m. ex Doncaster was worked, the trains worked were the 10.51 a.m. ex Doncaster, and the 5.40 p.m. ex Kings Cross, the engine working being altered to allow this.

The weights of trains shown are those leaving terminals; they were altered slightly en route, but the ton miles have been corrected for this.

Coal Consumption

The coal was weighed on and off daily at Doncaster, and at Ferme Park when required, representatives from the Chief Mechanical Engineer's and Running Dept being present.

The amounts of coal required for lighting up from cold water after washing out, and from warm water, were found from tests with both engines. The amount of coal required between

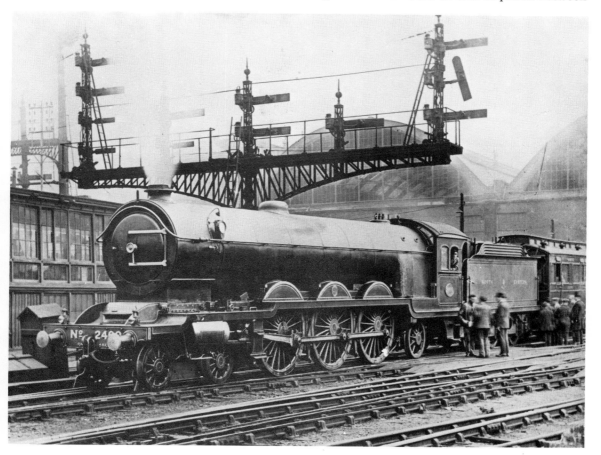

The Pacific engine trials of 1923: Raven Pacific No 2400 then unnamed, and lettered 'North Eastern', ready to leave Kings Cross with the 5.40 pm Leeds express

trains at Kings Cross was also found and these amounts deducted from the total, leaving that actually used on the trip.

Water Consumption

The tender of engine 1472 was metered inch by inch, and checked by weighing. Meters were fitted to the water side of each injector, but they did not prove satisfactory in operation.

The tender of engine 2400 was metered out inch by inch by a special meter, the property of the Darlington Corporation Water Co. which had only recently been checked.

The consumption of water during the run was obtained by a special dipping pipe in the tender in connection with a water column in the dynamometer car. Air forced into the system causes the water column to rise to the same height as the water in the tender.

It will be noted that on three trips water figures are not shown. Reliance was being placed on the injector meters, which were found afterwards to be unreliable in action, and the dipping pipe was not satisfactory on one trip.

Weather

The velocity and direction of wind were taken from the mid-day readings at Peterboro'.

Record No.	Dates	Train	No. of inter-mediate stops	No. of checks	Distance in miles	Time Minutes Booked	Time Minutes Actual	Speeds mph Booked	Speeds mph Actual	Tra Vehicl
									ENGINE No. 147	
946	June 25th	10.51 am Ex Doncaster	3	2	156.06	176	179.23	53.3	52.2	13
947	,, ,,	5.40 pm ,, Kings Cross	2	6	155.99	180	179.41	52.0	52.18	16
956	July 2nd	10.51 am ,, Doncaster	3	4	156.05	176	169.48	53.2	55.2	12
957	,, ,,	5.40 pm ,, Kings Cross	2	4	155.97	180	173.41	52.0	54.0	16
958	,, 3rd	10.51 am ,, Doncaster	3	2	156.05	176	172.88	53.2	54.1	13
959	,, ,,	5.40 pm ,, Kings Cross	2	5	156.02	180	172.38	52.0	54.2	16
Averages									53.7	
									ENGINE No. 240	
951	June 28th	12.52 pm Ex Doncaster	2	5	156.05	180	180.16	52.0	51.98	12
952	,, ,,	5.40 pm ,, Kings Cross	2	4	155.98	180	181.88	52.0	51.5	16
953	,, 29th	10.51 am ,, Doncaster	4	2	156.05	176	176.10	53.2	53.19	14
954	,, ,,	5.40 pm ,, Kings Cross	2	5	155.97	180	177.60	52.0	52.7	17
960	July 4th	10.51 am ,, Doncaster	4	1	156.06	176	172.15	53.2	54.4	14
961	,, ,,	5.40 pm ,, Kings Cross	2	4	156.00	180	173.26	52.0	54.0	16
Averages									53.0	

COMPARATIVE TESTS BETWEEN PACIFIC ENGINES MADE

Record No.	Water on trip Gallons Total	per mile	per hour	Per 1000 engine & train ton miles	Per 1000 train ton miles	Pounds per drawbar horse power hour	Pounds per sq foot of heating surface per hour	Total	Lighting up and at London	On trip	Base Per 100 engine & train ton mile
											ENGINE No. 147
946	—	—	—	—	—	—	—	14750	1120	13630	79.9
947	—	—	—	—	—	—	—				
956	6031	38.65	2137	68.1	92.4	29.7	6.18	16692	1120	15570	87.2
957	5347	34.5	1852	52.0	67.2	28.7	5.36				
958	6468	41.5	2247	66.5	87.4	29.3	6.50	17783	1456	16327	89.2
959	6022	38.6	2090	59.0	76.4	30.3	6.07				
Averages	5967	38.3	2081	61.4	80.8	31.0	6.03	16407	1232	15176	85.4
											ENGINE No. 240
951	4833	31.0	1611	52.3	69.6	30.7	5.60	17696	1456	16240	90.6
952	—	—	—	—	—	—	—				
953	6309	40.8	2151	65.0	85.3	31.65	7.43	17778	1120	16658	87.4
954	6994	44.6	2362	65.6	83.8	32.73	8.21				
960	7132	45.7	2489	73.7	96.7	32.3	8.65	19488	1456	18032	98.1
961	6225	39.8	2155	61.1	79.1	31.55	7.50				
Averages	6298	40.4	2153	63.5	82.9	31.7	7.48	18321	1344	16976	92.03

The table headed 'Sheet 1' gives details of performance on the six trips run with each engine on which the complete round was under observation. The coal consumption in each case covered the entire 312 miles from Doncaster to Kings Cross and back. These are summarised in the separate table, which shows that although the North Eastern engine returned a higher superheat temperature, and only a slightly higher evaporation, the Great Northern engine had a marked superiority in coal consumption per drawbar horsepower hour of 3.94 lb against 4.29. Special reference was made in the report

to the climbing from Kings Cross to Potters Bar, on the northbound runs; and here, although some very fine work was done by both engines, the advantage lay with No 1472. Her average time of 20.4 min for the 12.7 miles, with an average tare load of 519 tons, may be compared with 21.5 min with an average load of 527 tons. The respective average equivalent drawbar horsepowers are 1064 and 1002. Even so, like the Battle of Waterloo, it was 'a near-run thing'. As was so often the case in dynamometer car trials conducted on service trains the overall results did not give the complete picture as to

ETWEEN DONCASTER AND KINGS CROSS JUNE–JULY 1923										
at departure		Actual 1000 ton miles		Average drawbar pull tons	Average drawbar horse power	Average super heat	Average boiler pressure	Average steam chest pressure	Average cut off %	Weather
Axles	Tons	Engine and train	Train only							
GN SECTION										Fine each day
56	415.85	83.41	63.19	1.76	549	526	154	100	40	Wind 4 mph SE
70	518.85	100.78	77.56	1.96	610	543	162	113	38	
52	376.85	88.57	65.35	2.18	718	542	169	128	40	„ 6 „ SW
70	520.85	102.84	79.62	2.00	645	—	167	112	40	
62	452.85	97.28	74.06	2.36	763	563	165	129	40	„ 16 „ SW
70	515.85	102.12	78.90	2.17	702	560	168	124	40	
		95.83	73.11	2.07	663	547	164	118	40	
NE SECTION										
52	395.85	93.26	70.16	1.71	529	565	197	94	40	Wind 4 mph W
70	517.85	102.10	79.00	2.15	661	585	195	115	40	
62	452.85	97.06	73.96	2.14	679	572	198	105	40	„ 2 „ W
74	545.85	106.51	83.41	2.29	722	576	200	110	40	
62	452.85	96.75	73.75	2.37	771	566	200	125	40	„ 10 „ SW
70	515.85	101.86	78.76	2.12	683	582	194	91	40	
		97.92	76.5	2.13	673	574	197	106	40	

Pounds of Houghton main coal used										Evaporation	
on total coal used		Based on coal used on trip							Feed water temperature deg. F.	Pounds of water per pound of coal	
Per 1000 train ton miles	Per mile	Per 1000 engine & train ton miles	Per 1000 train ton miles	Per mile	Per hour	Per drawbar horse power hour	Per sq ft of heating surface per hour	Per sq ft of grate per hour		Actual	From & at 212°F
GN SECTION											
104.8	47.3	74.0	96.9	43.7	2280	3.92	0.613	54.8	61.0 / 60.0	—	—
115.02	53.5	81.5	107.5	49.9	2750	4.00	0.789	66.0	60.5 / 61.0	7.3	9.51
116.3	57.0	81.9	106.75	52.3	2845	3.89	0.821	74.8	61.0 / 61.5	7.65	10.8
112.04	52.6	79.13	103.71	48.6	2625	3.94	0.741	65.2	61.0	7.47	10.15
NE SECTION											
118.6	56.7	83.1	108.9	52.04	2765	4.52	0.936	64.9	62.5 / 62.5	—	—
113.0	56.99	81.9	105.9	53.4	2850	4.04	0.966	66.6	61.0 / 61.0	7.98	10.56
127.6	62.43	90.8	118.1	57.8	3161	4.31	1.088	75.5	61.5 / 61.0	7.42	9.8
120.4	58.71	85.26	110.96	54.41	2925	4.29	0.995	68.9	61.6	7.7	10.18

what happened on some individual runs, and the final up journey of the Raven 'Pacific' was an outstanding effort.

LNER PACIFIC ENGINE TRIALS
Average results for all tests: June and July 1923

ENGINE NO	1472	2400
SECTION	GN	NE
Average speed mph	53.7	53.0
Actual 1000 ton miles (train only)	73.11	76.5
Average dbh	663.0	673.0
Superheat °F	547.0	574.0
Boiler pressure psi	164.0	197.0
Steam chest pressure psi	118.0	106.0
Cut off, per cent	40.0	40.0
Water: gal per mile	38.3	40.4
lb per dbh hr	31.0	31.7
Coal: lb per mile (inclusive)	52.6	58.7
lb per mile (exclusive of lighting up)	48.6	54.4
lb per dbh hr	3.94	4.29
lb per sq ft of grate area per hr	65.2	68.9
Evaporation: feed water, temperature °F	61.0	61.6
lb of water per lb of coal	7.47	7.7
gal of water per hr used	2081	2153

From certain of the dynamometer car records as have been preserved detailed logs of two journeys have been prepared. On the basis of these two runs alone the honours were emphatically with the North Eastern. In saying so however I must add that this was the day on which No 1472 was unable to make the return test trip, because of an overheated side-rod bush. From the very start however the engine was

barely holding her own. For the North Eastern men it was their last trip to London, and they signalised it in no uncertain style. Except between Retford and Grantham they gained handsomely on schedule time, and although they were a little late on leaving Peterborough they made a magnificent run up to Kings Cross. Throughout from Doncaster they were doing substantially better than their rival on all the uphill stretches. It may have been that the Great Northern driver on No 1472 was indulging in a little 'coal-dodging' on his own account, and in the absence of any further detailed logs of performance during the test period I have included in this table of comparative performance a run observed by Mr Cecil J. Allen, from the footplate, on engine No 1473, in the spring of 1923, which shows the Great Northern design of 'Pacific' to very much greater advantage, albeit with a load lighter by one coach throughout. It was significant however, in view of the valve setting originally provided on these engines, that the cut-off was never reduced below 40 per cent either on 1472 or 1473. Even considering the vastly better work of 1473 over 1472, as shown in the tables, the former engine 'had nothing', to use a colloquialism, over the more heavily worked North Eastern engine when Driver Blades and Fireman Fisher were on their truly top form.

On the overall results of the trials between 1472 and 2400, as shown in the table (this page),

Gresley and Raven Pacifics alongside: No 2403 *City of Durham* and No 2571 *Sunstar*

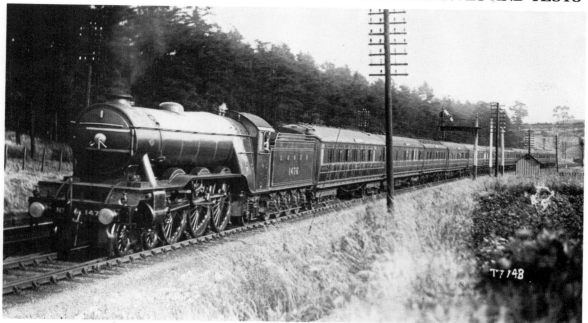

Down Newcastle express near Ganwick signal box, hauled by 4—6—2 No 1476, afterwards No 4476
Royal Lancer

LNER 10.51 AM DONCASTER—PETERBOROUGH

Run No Engine 4—6—2 No Railway Load, tons E/F			1 1472 GN			2 2400 NE			3 1473 GN		
to Grantham				453/485			453/485			413/440	
to Kings Cross				483/520			483/520			448/480	
Dist miles		Sch min	Actual m s		Speeds mph	Actual m s		Speeds mph	Actual m s		Speeds mph
0.0	DONCASTER . .		0 00		—	0 00		—	0 00		—
4.7	Rossington . . .		7 36		50½	7 07		53	8 20		56½
6.5	*Milepost 149½* . .		9 55		45	9 11		51½	10 35		51
8.3	Bawtry . . .		12 01		58	11 05		66	12 20		66
12.1	Ranskill . .		15 41		63	14 24		68	15 40		70½
17.4	RETFORD . .	21	21 27			20 36			21 15		
4.9	*Markham Box* . .		8 48		39½	8 27		41½	8 00		48
6.7	Tuxford . .		10 53		59	10 31		60	9 50		—
11.2	Crow Park . .		14 58		75	14 25		74	13 35		80½
12.2	Carlton . .		15 49		69	15 11		70	14 20		80½
18.5	NEWARK . . .	21	21 23		64	21 17			19 35		68
—			—			0 00			sig stop		
23.2	Claypole . .		26 04		58	7 29		53	28 10		
27.1	Hougham . .		30 17		53	11 39		56	33 00		55½
28.9	Barkston . .		32 32		42½	13 43		50	35 05		47½
33.1	GRANTHAM . .	38	38 30			19 25			40 50		
3.5	Great Ponton . .		8 30		35	7 05		40	6 35		44
5.4	*Stoke Box* . .		12 02		35	10 01		43½	9 10		46
8.4	Corby . .		15 23		65	13 05		65	12 20		68
13.3	Little Bytham .		19 36		74	17 12		76½	16 20		80½
16.9	Essendine . .		22 25		77	19 55		79	19 00		82
20.7	Tallington . .		25 31		74	22 56		74½	22 00		75
26.0	*Werrington Jc* . .		—			—			26 30		
29.1	PETERBOROUGH .	33	34 00			31 27			30 25		

THE GRESLEY PACIFICS

				LNER 12.31 PM PETERBOROUGH–KINGS CROSS					
Run No			1		2		3		
Engine 4—6—2 No			1472		2400		1473		
Railway			GN		NE		GN		
Load, tons E/F			483/520		483/520		448/480		
Dist miles		Sch min	Actual m s	Speeds mph	Actual m s	Speeds mph	Actual m s	Speeds mph
---	---	---	---	---	---	---	---	---
0.0	PETERBOROUGH	0	0 00	—	0 00	—	0 00	—
1.4	*Fletton Jc*		—	—	3 37	36	3 15	40½
3.8	Yaxley		6 33	53	6 39	51½	6 25	—
7.0	Holme		9 47	63	9 55	62½	9 50	59
12.9	Abbots Ripton		15 45	50½	16 00	49½	16 25	50
14.4	*Milepost 62*		17 37	—	17 52	47½	18 15	48
17.5	HUNTINGDON	20	20 36	↳ 68	20 50	73	21 20	70½
20.4	Offord		23 10	68	23 16	73	24 00	
24.7	St Neots		27 18	56	27 04	60	28 10	56½
28.9	Tempsford		31 31	63	31 03	65½	32 15	64½
32.3	Sandy		34 51	58/61	34 13	62½	35 30	60
35.3	Biggleswade		37 51	59	37 03	63	38 30	60
39.4	Arlesey		42 19	57	41 13	61	42 50	54
40.7	Three Counties		43 43	57	42 29	59½	44 10	61½
44.5	HITCHIN	48	48 07	47½	46 34	51	48 15	—
47.8	Stevenage		52 46	42	50 55	44½	52 20	48
51.4	Knebworth		57 06	49	55 04	51	56 20	—
—			sigs		—		—	
54.4	Welwyn		61 06	36	58 18	—	59 30	
58.7	HATFIELD	64	66 41	56	62 04	71	63 20	74
63.7	Potters Bar		72 43	49½	66 51	61	68 35	53½
67.2	New Barnet		75 40	65	69 58	74½	71 55	70½
71.4	Wood Green		81 16		73 35	73½	75 20	77½
73.9	Finsbury Park		83 47	(check)	75 38	68½	77 25	
76.4	KINGS CROSS	84	87 37	*	79 24		81 25	

*84 min net

1.30 pm down Leeds express passing Finsbury Park hauled by engine No 1478 N, afterwards 4478 *Hermit*

Engine No 4472 *Flying Scotsman* specially painted and embellished for the British Empire Exhibition at Wembley in 1924

Gresley was justified in recommending the adoption of his own 'Pacific' design as the future LNER standard, and orders were placed for forty further engines of the class—twenty with the North British Locomotive Co Ltd, and twenty with Doncaster Works. The last engine of the 1923 Doncaster batch, No 1481, had been built with reduced height of boiler mountings and cab to suit the loading gauge of the North British section, and the forty new engines authorised after the 1923 trials were built to the reduced heights thus required.

Engine No. 1478 N, ready to leave Kings Cross with the 5.40 pm Leeds express

THE GRESLEY PACIFICS

Before any of these new engines took the road a very important exposition of LNER locomotive prowess had begun, in the British Empire exhibition at Wembley, opened by His Majesty King George V in May 1924. Each of the British main line railways staged a notable exhibit, and in that of the LNER the centre-piece was a Gresley 'Pacific'. The two original Great Northern members of the class were already named, and so a third, No 1472, was, like the Ivatt 'Atlantic' No 1442 in 1910, given a new special exhibition finish and named *Flying Scotsman*. A handsome souvenir brochure was prepared, containing a portfolio of working drawings and a complete specification, and this brochure included details of the test running of the engine in the previous year, though not to the extent of including also those of her North Eastern rival. But this brochure is interesting in another respect. I have referred in the previous chapter to the suspension, and how that of the coupled wheels was not entirely satisfactory. It is generally understood that the helical springs on the driving axle were changed to the laminated type early in the history of the class, even on the Doncaster batch built in 1923, namely 1472 to 1481; but in this brochure, issued in 1924, not only does the general arrangement drawing show helical springs under the centre pair of coupled wheels, but the specification clearly states: 'The engine is suspended independently at each axle. Helical springs are used on the bogie and driving wheels, and laminated on the leading and trailing coupled wheels, the trailing carrying wheels and the tender wheels.' I have however been able to ascertain recently that the change was made before engine No 4472 was built, and that the references in the brochure were a 'carry-over' from the original specification of No 1470. So far as the tender was concerned, I have seen it stated that the *Flying Scotsman* exhibited at Wembley did not have attached to it the standard tender, and that as space was limited a 6-wheeled tender was substituted. Most photographs I have seen of the engine in the exhibition show clearly the standard tender, with the new number 4472, but one picture does show a six-wheel tender off a K3, so it had both at different times.

CHAPTER 4

LNER STANDARD

The decision to build a further forty Gresley 'Pacifics' was taken in order to provide for working the East Coast Route between London and Edinburgh, together with the West Riding expresses on the Great Northern section entirely with 'Pacifics'. The original allocation was all except one of the Doncaster-built batch, Nos 2543–61, to the Great Northern; five to the North British, Nos 2563–7, and the remaining sixteen to the North Eastern, namely 2562 and 2568–82. Thus when all these engines were in service the Great Northern had thirty-one, the

North Eastern sixteen, and the North British five. As the new standard engines came into service lineside observers noted them attached temporarily as it turned out, to several unusual sheds. For instance No 2563, the first of those built by the North British Locomotive Company, was at Eastfield, and the second of that batch went at first to St Margarets. At roughly the same time four of the Doncaster built engines, Nos 2547, 2548, 2550 and 2551 went to Gorton, Great Central Section. With the exception of No 2563 which was named when

The second of the 'general service' Pacifics of 1924, No. 2544, afterwards named *Lemberg*

51

General service 'Pacific' No 2553, as originally built, later named *Manna*, and afterwards *Prince of Wales*

new *William Whitelaw*, after the chairman of the LNER, all the new engines as well as Nos 4473–81 of the original Doncaster batch of 1923 were unnamed. When going into regular main line traffic they were distributed between six sheds only: Kings Cross, Grantham, Doncaster, Gateshead, Heaton and Haymarket.

Although the design was standard in its broadest sense there were a number of points of detail on which individual groups of engines differed. The reduced height of cabs and boiler mountings on the 2543–82 series has already been mentioned, and in my opinion the appearance of the engines was improved by the change. This, of course, was quite superficial; but then there was the matter of brakes. The five engines attached to the North British section were, like their Great Northern counterparts fitted only with the vacuum brake. Presumably their running was confined solely to East Coast trains, which were composed entirely of dual fitted stock. The Reid 'Atlantics' and other NBR engines used on Anglo-Scottish trains were fitted with both vacuum and Westinghouse. The

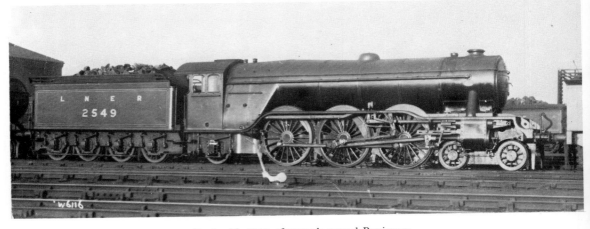

Engine No 2549, afterwards named *Persimmon*

North Eastern, on the other hand, was a purely Westinghouse line and the fifteen engines 2568 to 2582 had the Westinghouse and no other.

There was a further complication over the brake equipment on these new standard 'Pacifics'. For many years the North Eastern had used the Raven system of fog signalling. This consisted of an arm in the four-foot, rather like the trip arm of a train stop on the London Underground Lines, which was raised when the associated signal was at danger and made contact with a pendant device on the locomotive, as shown in the accompanying photograph. The raising of the shoe actuated a valve which caused a whistle to sound in the engine cab. It was installed on the main line between York (Skelton Junction) and Croxdale, 60 miles of double track, and between Forest Hall and Alnmouth, a further 30 route miles. Prior to grouping the North Eastern Railway had some 1400 locomotives equipped, and the running department set such store upon its value, that for a time all new locomotives allocated to the North Eastern Area after grouping were equipped. On the purely North Eastern engines compressed air from the brake system was used to sound the whistle and the 'Pacifics' 2568–2582

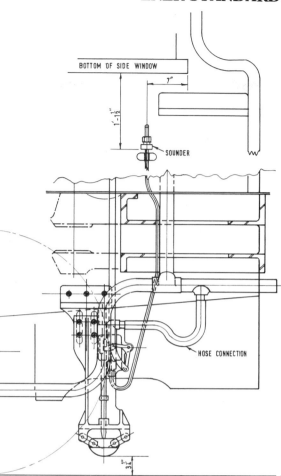

Layout of NE Area cab signal equipment on engines fitted with vacuum and steam brake

were fitted with the standard NER arrangement. But the vacuum-braked engines stationed in Scotland, and the Doncaster-built engine No 2562 had a modified arrangement to enable a vacuum siren to be used. This is shown on the accompanying drawing, which was prepared from a Darlington drawing dated November 1923. From 1930 onwards, when the vacuum brake had been standardised over the LNER many Westinghouse fitted engines were converted to steam brakes, for the engine and tender, and a number of 'Pacifics' working in the North Eastern Area had a modified form of fog signalling, on which the whistle was operated by vacuum when running trains, and by steam when working light, or on unbraked goods trains. The replacement of semaphore signals north of Skelton Junction by colour light signals in 1934 was accompanied by the removal of the track

Hanging bracket and plunger of NER cab signal equipment

arms, and the system of fog signalling that had served the NER so well for so many years passed out of use.

The allocation of the Gresley 'Pacific' engines to the North Eastern Area did not receive a wholesale welcome from the men. There were many features of the cab layout and equipment that were strange to them, and with many of the older men there was some resentment that their own engines had been passed over in favour of those from the Great Northern. Although the two railways had been allies for many years it did mean that neither approved of equipment long standard on the other! The East Coast schedules north of York were not exacting, and for some little time they were not improved by the lackadaisical methods of North Eastern drivers working the Gresley 'Pacifics'. That they did little better with the Raven 'Pacifics' is perhaps beside the point. There would be no significance in relating details of runs made in these early days; the trouble was psychological rather than technical, and I shall tell later in this book how successfully the early prejudices were overcome. In the meantime Gresley and his 'Pacifics' were being faced with a challenge of a different kind that some commentators have attributed to the first year of the British Empire Exhibition.

For a brief period the Gresley and Raven Pacifics were, on the basis of nominal tractive effort, the most powerful express passenger locomotives in Great Britain; but that distinction was snatched from them in August 1923 when the first of the Great Western 'Castles' was completed at Swindon. Many visitors to the Wembley Exhibition, who saw *Caerphilly Castle* and *Flying Scotsman* sitting back to back, felt that the Great Western claim to pre-eminence was one of statistics only and that a 'Castle' could not hope to compete on level terms with an engine whose boiler and firebox were so much larger. After all, Churchward himself had said that the boiler was the principal problem on a locomotive. In view of so overt a challenge, albeit in circumstances entirely static, the discerning onlooker could well imagine the LNER management saying to the Great Western, in as many words: 'You claim to have the most powerful express passenger locomotive; well, prove it!' Among the rank and file of the GWR it was certainly understood that the 'challenge' had come from the LNER. This however was not the case. Sir Felix Pole, the dynamic general manager of the GWR never let slip an opportunity to publicise the equipment and achievement of his railway, and the suggestion of a friendly interchange of locomotives was made at a private luncheon party with Sir Ralph Wedgwood, of the LNER. One can be fairly sure that the idea appealed also to William Whitelaw the chairman of the LNER who, in

The 1925 Locomotive Exchange: GWR 4—6—0 No 4079 *Pendennis Castle* and 4—6—2 No 4475 *Flying Fox* at Kings Cross Shed

The 10 am down Scotch express passing Holloway South hauled by engine No 2545 *Diamond Jubilee*

the past, had engineered more locomotive exchanges than any man living. One recalls:

1. Highland 'Castle' class 4—6—0 *versus* NBR 'intermediate' 4—4—0.
2. NBR 'Atlantic' *versus* LNWR 'Experiment' 4—6—0 between Preston and Carlisle.
3. NBR 'Atlantic' *versus* a Midland compound, and an NER 4-cylinder compound 'Atlantic' over the Waverley Route.
4. A North Eastern 3-cylinder 0—8—0 *versus* a Great Western '28XX' 2—8—0 on the Glenfarg bank of the NBR between Perth and Kinross Junction.

In 1925 the designers of the locomotives were perhaps less enthusiastic than their respective general managers though the suggestion I have seen printed elsewhere that Gresley was not consulted, and learned first of the forthcoming exchange from the newspapers is pure rubbish. Collett had astonished the locomotive world, almost into disbelief, with a paper to the World Power Conference, in which he disclosed results of dynamometer car test runs with the second of the 'Castle' class engines, and felt that was publicity enough. Gresley was not entirely satisfied with the performance of the 'Pacifics', and at the very time the Interchange with the Great Western was launched Doncaster Works was engaged on some experimental work of its own. On the Great Western side, whether

Collett liked it or not, the whole thing was taken up with tremendous gusto. For the LNER it was perhaps unfortunate that the enginemen concerned came from Kings Cross shed; for while A. Pibworth, who was chosen to run on the GWR, was an enterprising and resourceful driver, his counterpart Ben Glasgow, who represented the LNER on its own road was a 'safe' and cautious man, not only a little over-awed by the occasion, but dogged with bad luck in the engines allocated to him. Kings Cross then had only two of the original batch of 'Pacifics', 4474 and 4475; by April 1925 these had been re-inforced by four of the new standard engines, 2545, 2546, 2552 and 2553. No 4474, always an excellent engine, and at that time still unnamed, was chosen to go to the GWR, and 4475 recently named *Flying Fox* was the choice for the 'home' running. To everyone's disappointment the LNER had a bad week. *Flying Fox* failed with a hot box on her very first down trip, and when No 2545 was substituted she too was in trouble, and throughout the tests failed to rise barely to normal 'Pacific' standards of running.

The principle source of interest from the LNER point of view was the running of 4474. With her crew went E. D. Trask, who later came to hold high office as locomotive running superintendent, first in the Scottish and then in the Southern Area of the LNER. On the GWR

The LNER 4—6—2 No 4474 approaching Reading with the 1.30 pm West of England express during the week of preliminary running

THE 1925 LOCOMOTIVE EXCHANGE

Up Cornish Riviera Express entering Paddington hauled by LNER 4—6—2 No 4474

their immediate guide and philosopher was the celebrated chief locomotive inspector G. H. Flewellyn, and once Trask had been over the route with him, on Great Western engines, they began the week of preliminary road-learning, with no one but a pilotman to guide them, on the easily timed 1.30 pm from Paddington, with engine No 4474. Very soon they were in dead trouble. The fireman started to build up as though he was using hard Yorkshire coal, and the boiler pressure went plummeting down. Even the imperturbable Driver Pibworth was alarmed; but Trask quickly realised that firing Welsh coal in huge lumps was leaving gaps in the fire and letting in air from the ashpan without its being used for combustion, and he set about breaking coal into small pieces. Many years later he told me he spent most of that first run in the tender breaking coal!

The 'Pacific' chassis did not take too kindly to the twists and turns of the line, particularly that part of it west of Newton Abbot. When they arrived at Plymouth and had in due course worked down to Laira shed, Trask was met by a running foreman bubbling over with ill-concealed joy, who said at once: 'It looks as if I have won my bet.' Trask asked what he meant, and the reply came: 'Look at your left hand big end! I bet that if you ever got here you'd never get back!' The outside of that big-end was certainly plastered with white metal, but it did not seem unduly hot, and examination over a pit showed that all was well. As to that spattering of white metal, Trask laughingly explained that they had merely shaved off a bit of the end of the bush, and he added 'We've now got the lateral clearance we need for your damned curves!' It is of course, well known that the Gresley 'Pacifics' built at Doncaster had fairly generous clearances, particularly in lateral movement, and that those built by the North British Locomotive Company, and provided with more conventional clearances had to be modified after their first delivery. After that first run down to Plymouth no trouble was experienced with 4474; and once the fireman was used to it she steamed freely enough on soft Welsh coal. Her crew, with Trask at their elbows, had a week to learn the road, and then on 27 April 1925, with no one except Driver Manning of Old Oak Common, as pilotman with them, they took out the down Cornish Riviera Express.

There is no need for me to emphasise the difficulty of working that famous train, when the tare load out of Paddington was 500 tons,

LNER STANDARD

GWR VERSUS LNER INTERCHANGE TRIALS: 1925
Engine No 4474
Driver : A. Pibworth : Fireman : E. Birkwood

Date		April 27	May 1
Load, tons E/F			
to Westbury		499/530	496/530
to Taunton		427/455	424/455
to Exeter		364/390	361/390
to Plymouth		292/310	292/310

Dist miles		Sch min	Actual m s	Actual m s
0.0	Paddington	0	0 00	0 00
9.1	Southall	11	13 15	12 55
18.5	Slough	20	22 01	22 05
24.2	Maidenhead	25½	27 14	27 30
36.0	Reading	37	37 52	38 50
53.1	Newbury	56	56 43	58 15
66.4	Bedwyn	69½	70 08	72 05
70.1	Savernake		74 25	76 20
95.6	Westbury	97½	98 30	100 20
108.5	Milepost 122¾		116 06	116 10
115.3	Castle Cary	120	122 21	121 50
137.9	Cogload Jc	143	143 07	142 05
142.9	Taunton	148	147 49	147 00
153.8	Whiteball Box		160 42	161 20
173.7	Exeter	179	178 37	180 50
—			pws	pws
193.9	Newton Abbot	203	202 16	203 15
			pws	pws
197.7	Dainton Box	209½	209 54	210 30
202.5	Totnes	215½	215 49	216 25
209.4	Brent	225	227 50	227 05
219.0	Hemerdon Box	237	239 00	237 30
224.2	Lipson Jc	245	—	243 15
			pws	pws
225.7	Plymouth	247	248 01	246 45

or very nearly so; when the maximum 'Castle' load of eight 70 ft coaches had to be taken over the South Devon line, and there were the implications of slip coach working to be mastered by a strange driver. It was, without any question, the hardest task then set daily to any British express locomotive crew. The return working with a train of no more than 324 tons tare, from Exeter was an easy job by comparison. The accompanying table gives summary details of the runs made on 27 April and 1 May, the latter hindered somewhat by a strong adverse wind; but on 27 April, to pass Exeter on time was a very remarkable feat of enginemanship, as well as a demonstration of the capacity of the Gresley 'Pacifics' in their original form, with the original valve gear. Early in the week Gresley went over to Paddington to meet them in, and he asked Trask how they were doing. 'All right,' came the reply, 'but not so well as the GW.'

'Oh, but you must,' was Gresley's quick rejoinder, to which Trask countered with: 'I don't see how we can. They've got a better valve gear than ours.'

57

THE GRESLEY PACIFICS

Gresley then reminded him: 'Mr Wintour [locomotive works manager at Doncaster] is getting out a modified form of ours', to which Trask replied 'Well that won't be much good to us this week!' And Gresley I regret to add, turned on his heel and walked away.

I need not recall the acrimonious exchanges that took place between the two railway companies, following a lengthy and somewhat biased account of the whole interchange that was published in the Great Western Railway Magazine. But the plain fact remained that in the running between Kings Cross and Doncaster the LNER was as unlucky, both in its engines and personnel, as it had been fortunate in the representatives who went on to the GWR. As a result the LNER was soundly beaten on its own metals. It could have been a different story had some of the 'crack' Doncaster crews of that period, with their regular engines, been given the chance of competing. Runs logged by various observers in 1924 and 1925 showed vastly better work than was done on the specific trains set aside for the interchange running.

The official figures for the coal consumption on the LNER line were as follows:
It was on 27 April that the LNER engine No 4475 failed, and on this account the comparative GWR consumption on 28 April was not included in the records. It must be conceded that in consideration of the relatively moderate scheduled speeds of the test trains, the coal consumption of both engines was high, especially

Duty : 10.10 am Kings Cross to Grantham and back : COAL IN LB PER TRAIN MILE			
GWR No 4079*	55.7	55.9	59.4
LNER No 2545†	59.6	58.1	59.2

*27 and 29 April; 1 May respectively
†28 and 30 April; 2 May respectively

Duty : 1.30 pm Kings Cross to Doncaster and back : COAL IN LB PER TRAIN MILE		
LNER †	54.1	56.5
GWR No 4079 *	48.8	50.7

†29 April and 1 May respectively
*30 April and 2 May respectively

on the runs to Grantham and back. On the down Cornish Riviera Express the successive figures, with the LNE and GW engine on alternate days, were 50.0, 44.1, 48.8, 45.6, 52.4 and 46.8 lb per mile, with a more pronounced advantage to the GW engine. Even so the LNER engine crew did a remarkable job, seeing that the longest non-stop runs then performed by Pacific engines at Kings Cross shed were no more than 105.5 miles, and that No 4474 was required to run 225.7 miles in the 'exchange' with all the awkward conditions of the South Devon line coming right at the end. On balance

Up Cornish Riviera Express near Acton, hauled by LNER 4—6—2 No 4474

General service 'Pacific' No 2552, later named *Sansovino*, at Kings Cross Top Shed

the Great Western undoubtedly had the best of it in this single week of running; equally, it was the losers who came to benefit most by the experience.

Before coming to the important changes in the details of 'Pacific' design that eventuated I must set on record some of the finest runs made by engines in their original condition. It was also in 1925 and 1926 that the majority of the class received the names by which they subsequently became so well known, and these are set out below.

1. ORIGINAL DONCASTER ENGINES

4470	Great Northern	4476	Royal Lancer
4471	Sir Frederick Banbury	4477	Gay Crusader
4472	Flying Scotsman	4478	Hermit
4473	Solario	4479	Robert the Devil
4474	Victor Wild	4480	Enterprise
4475	Flying Fox	4481	St. Simon

2. GENERAL SERVICE ENGINES: DONCASTER BUILT

2543	Melton	2553	Prince of Wales *
2544	Lemberg	2554	Woolwinder
2545	Diamond Jubilee	2555	Centenary
2546	Donovan	2556	Ormonde
2547	Doncaster	2557	Blair Atholl
2548	Galtee More	2558	Tracery
2549	Persimmon	2559	The Tetrarch
2550	Blink Bonny	2560	Pretty Polly
2551	Prince Palatine	2562	Isinglass

*originally Manna

From 1925 onwards I was working near Kings Cross station and I saw a good deal of the goings and comings of these engines, as well as making a number of journeys up and down the line. One certainly formed the impression that they were not so reliable as 'publicity' would have had us believe. One afternoon I went down to Peterborough on the 1.30 pm Leeds express, loaded to 510 tons gross behind the tender, and engine No 2553 *Prince of Wales* seemed definitely weak on the banks. We took no less than $24\frac{1}{4}$ min to pass Potters Bar, having fallen to 36 mph as early as New Barnet; Hatfield was passed 5 min late (29 min 55 sec from Kings Cross) and although we held our own afterwards the arrival at Peterborough was $4\frac{1}{4}$ min late ($87\frac{1}{4}$ min from Kings Cross). On another occasion with the same train with a 535-ton load, No 2543 *Melton*, was steaming very poorly.

3. GENERAL SERVICE ENGINES: NB Loco Built

2563	William Whitelaw	2573	Harvester
2564	Knight of the Thistle	2574	St Frusquin
2565	Merrie Hampton	2575	Galopin
2566	Ladas	2576	The White Knight
2567	St Visto	2577	Night Hawk
2568	Sceptre	2578	Bayardo
2569	Gladiateur	2579	Dick Turpin
2570	Tranquil	2580	Shotover
2571	Sunstar	2581	Neil Gow
2572	St Gatien	2582	Sir Hugo

An interesting photograph showing engine No 2553, working a down express past Holloway in the short period she was named *Manna*

We fell to 32 mph on the climb to Potters Bar; took 30¾ min to Hatfield, and could make no substantial speed afterwards. Indeed, on the racing descent past Hitchin we ran for some distance without steam, passing Three Counties at 56 mph! Schedule time was then 84 min, and we eventually pulled up at Peterborough in 93 min 20 sec.

On the up road I had a number of runs on the Leeds express due into Kings Cross at 5.10 pm, which was allowed 83 min from Peterborough, but the loads rarely exceeded 400 tons by very much. Engine No 2561 *Minoru* was frequently on this job, and she gave me a run up in 79 min 5 sec, with 420 tons, and another in 82 min 35 sec (81 min net) with 410 tons. But by far the best I had on this train with engines having the

original valve gear was yet another with *Minoru* when she was checked by signal at Stukeley Box, north of Huntingdon, and then driven with such vigour as to reach Kings Cross 4 min early. I have tabulated this run as a good example of the work of the original engines with a medium load. To restore something of the balance of reputation of these engines in their early days, so far as my own recording was concerned I must mention yet another run on the 1.30 pm with No 2553 *Prince of Wales* and a 475-ton load. We were going well up the long ascent to Potters Bar when we were slowed at Ganwick Box, between the Hadley and Potters Bar tunnels for permanent work, and were 2 min late through Hatfield in consequence. But some good work followed and we clocked

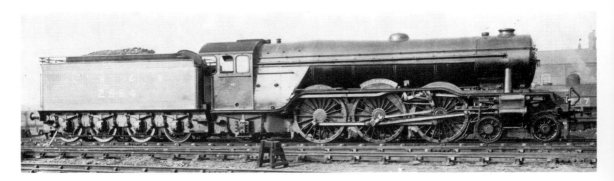

Engine No 2554, after being named *Woolwinder*

LNER 3.47 PM PETERBOROUGH–KINGS CROSS

Load: 396 tons tare, 425 tons full
Engine: 4—6—2 No 2561 *Minoru*

Dist miles		Sch min	Actual m s	Speeds mph
0.0	PETERBOROUGH	0	0 00	—
1.4	*Fletton Jc* . .		3 20	
7.0	Holme . .		9 20	67
12.9	Abbots Ripton .		15 10	53½
14.4	*Milepost 62* .		16 50	57½
—			sigs.	15
17.5	HUNTINGDON .	20	21 35	57½
20.4	Offord . .		24 30	64½
24.7	St Neots .		28 35	58½
28.9	Tempsford .		32 30	69
32.3	Sandy . .		35 35	64½
35.3	Biggleswade .		38 20	65
37.8	*Langford Bridge* .		40 45	59
40.7	Three Counties .		43 30	65
44.5	HITCHIN . .	47	47 20	56
47.8	Stevenage .		51 10	50
51.4	Knebworth .		55 00	60/55
54.4	Welwyn .		58 00	67
58.7	HATFIELD . .	63	61 45	75
63.7	Potters Bar .		66 35	60
67.2	New Barnet .		69 45	72½
71.4	Wood Green .		73 15	76½
73.8	Finsbury Park .		75 25	
76.4	KINGS CROSS .	83	79 00	

Net time 76½ min

into Peterborough 15 sec inside schedule. The sprint from Stevenage onwards included my first personal record of a maximum of 80 mph with one of these engines. The average speed over the 50 miles from Knebworth to Fletton Junction was 65 mph.

The even tenor of train working on all railways in Great Britain was much disturbed in 1926 by the prolonged coal strike following the General Strike; and on the LNER the haulage capacity of the Gresley 'Pacifics' was put severely to the test by the taking up of Gresley's own claim that they had been designed to work 600-ton trains. On one occasion No 2543 *Melton* brought a train of 630 tons from Peterborough to Kings Cross in 85 min despite an intermediate slack costing 2 min, while another engine of the class brought up the late evening Scotch express from Grantham to Kings Cross in 119 min also with a load of 630 tons. The only detailed log of a 600-ton run in this period was secured by Mr Cecil J. Allen, on a train having the generous allowance of 92 min from Peterborough to Kings Cross. It was not a very demanding occasion, and engine and crew dealt

LNER PETERBOROUGH–KINGS CROSS

Load: 576 tons tare 620 tons full
Engine: 4—6—2 No 4474 *Victor Wild*

Dist miles		Sch min	Actual m s	Speeds mph
0.0	PETERBOROUGH	0	0 00	—
1.4	*Fletton Jc* . .		3 26	
7.0	Holme . .		10 14	55
12.9	Abbots Ripton .		16 52	44
17.5	HUNTINGDON .	24	22 15	63½
24.7	St Neots .		29 34	49
28.9	Tempsford .		34 08	—
35.3	Biggleswade .		40 47	—
39.4	Arlesey .		45 23	49/55
44.5	HITCHIN . .	54	51 24	44
47.8	Stevenage .		56 13	37
58.7	HATFIELD . .	72	69 10	58
63.7	Potters Bar .		75 11	—
71.4	Wood Green .		83 16	58½
73.8	Finsbury Park .		86 06	
76.4	KINGS CROSS .	92	91 23	

Engine No 2546 *Donovan*

THE GRESLEY PACIFICS

with it adequately enough. The log is tabulated herewith as a record of an important period in Gresley 'Pacific' history, rather than an example of outstanding performance; from Stevenage onwards the engine was being worked under easy steam.

By far the finest run that I have ever seen with one of these engines having the original valve gear was one on the 5.45 pm Leeds express from Kings Cross, when the load, as far as Grantham was no less than 580 tons. There is no doubt that when in top form these engines could handle 600-ton loads on the fastest schedules then in operation, though in making the claim Gresley was almost certainly thinking in terms of 600-tons *tare*, which is the basic method of reckoning loads. On the run now coming into consideration the tare load was only 536 tons. It is tabulated in some detail, but further comment is necessary. The engine made an excellent start up the bank to Finsbury Park and then after reaching a maximum of 51½ mph at Wood Green there was a fall only to 44 mph in the ensuing 7¾ miles of 1 in 200 ascent to Potters Bar. The drawbar horsepower involved here would be about 1400. Fine running followed, with a maximum of 82 mph at Three Counties. This was considered something rather wonderful at the time with such a load, though naturally the gravitational effect of the train would have been providing around 110 horsepower to assist the locomotive! But once down

Dist miles		Sch min	Actual m s	Speeds mph
0.0	Kings Cross .	0	0 00	—
2.6	Finsbury Park .		7 11	
5.0	Wood Green .		10 41	51½
9.2	New Barnet .		16 03	—
12.7	Potters Bar .		20 57	44
17.7	HATFIELD .	25	26 07	69
22.0	Welwyn .		30 03	54 (min)
25.0	Knebworth .		33 17	—
28.6	Stevenage .		36 40	
31.9	HITCHIN .		39 31	—
35.7	Three Counties .		42 24	82
41.1	Biggleswade .		46 49	—
44.1	Sandy .		49 20	—
47.5	Tempsford .		52 17	—
51.7	St Neots .		56 14	60
56.0	Offord .		60 13	67
58.9	HUNTINGDON .		62 59	—
62.0	*Milepost 62* .		66 36	44
69.4	Holme .		73 48	71½
72.6	Yaxley .		76 43	
75.0	*Fletton Jc* .		79 10	
76.4	PETERBOROUGH .	83	81 24	
3.2	*Werrington Jc* .		6 40	
8.4	Tallington .		12 22	60
12.2	Essendine .		16 13	—
15.8	Little Bytham .		20 10	—
20.7	Corby .		26 22	46½/50
23.7	*Stoke Box* .		30 12	45
25.6	Great Ponton .		32 18	
29.1	GRANTHAM .	36	36 00	

into the level country the average speed over the undulating 32½ miles from Biggleswade to

Down Scotch express climbing Holloway bank hauled by No 4479 *Robert the Devil*

62

Engine No 2543 *Melton* on up Leeds express near Stevenage: engine still with short-travel valves, but number on cab side

LNER GRANTHAM—DONCASTER

Load: 502 tons tare 545 tons full
Engine: 4—6—2 No 4471 *Sir Frederick Banbury*

Dist miles				Actual m s	Speeds mph
0.0	GRANTHAM	.	.	0 00	
6.0	Hougham	.	.	8 53	
14.6	NEWARK	.	.	15 56	75
20.9	Carlton	.	.	21 21	—
28.2	*Markham Box*	.	.	29 26	47
33.1	RETFORD	.	.	34 24	68
38.4	Ranskill	.	.	39 38	67
42.2	Bawtry	.	.	43 12	49 (min)
45.8	Rossington	.	.	47 14	65
50.5	DONCASTER	.	.	52 54	

Yaxley, 65 mph, was of more significance, and involved an output of about 950 drawbar horsepower continuously. The train arrived at Peterborough $1\frac{1}{2}$ min early.

Continuing from Peterborough, still with a gross load of 580 tons, speed reached 60 mph at Tallington, and then fell away gradually to a sustained minimum of $46\frac{1}{2}$ mph on the 1 in 200 before Corby. Here the equivalent drawbar horsepower would have been about 1500. The difficult schedule of 36 min to Grantham was exactly kept. The detaching of the Lincoln coach reduced the load to 502 tons tare for the last stage of No 4471's run. Here with a gross load of 545 tons there was no difficulty in cutting schedule time by just over 2 min. This was a very fine run, though on the records available, and my own personal experiences with these very heavy trains I would regard it as distinctly exceptional.

Before leaving the early history of the Pacifics I must mention their experimental heavy freight equivalents, the 'P1' class 2—8—2 engines, No 2393 and 2394. These very handsome engines had boilers, cylinders and motion interchangeable with those of the Pacifics except that the valve gear was modified to provide 75 per cent cut-off in full gear, $5\frac{1}{2}$ in maximum valve travel, steam lap $1\frac{1}{4}$ in and exhaust lap $\frac{1}{8}$ in. For locomotives intended primarily for the heavy coal traffic between Peterborough and Ferme Park the coupled wheel diameter was large, 5 ft 2 in, and the nominal tractive effort was no more than 38,500 lb. But these engines were fitted also with a booster which provided an additional tractive effort of 8500 lb when in operation. In view of the high speeds attained by the Riddles 'BR9' 2—10—0s in more recent times, one wonders if Gresley had envisaged a mixed-traffic function for these 'P1' 2—8—2s at the time of their construction; but the only instance of which I have knowledge in which any express running was attempted was at the time the 'Cock o'the North' class 2—8—2 was under consideration. Then, one of the 'P1'

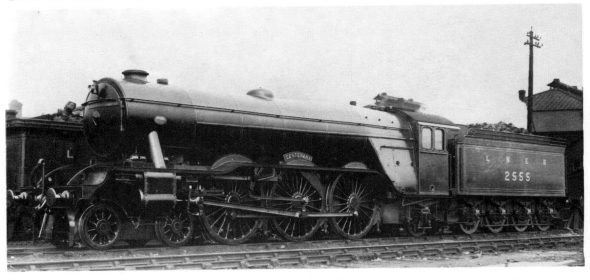

Engine No 2555 after being named *Centenary* but still with short travel valves, and number on tender

engines was put on to the semi-fast 8.45 am down from Kings Cross, under close observation, and a speed of 65 mph was easily attained. As freight engines, however, the 'P1' class was somewhat before its time, or more strictly had a haulage power greater than the freight train capacity of the line could accommodate.

The second of these engines, No 2394, was fitted with an 'E' type superheater, of the same proportions as that originally fitted to the 'Pacific' No 2562 *Isinglass*, as shown in the illustration (opposite page). Quite extensive tests were carried out in May 1926 between No 2562 and a standard engine with the 32-element Robinson superheater, No 2570 *Tranquil*. A total of twelve trips was made with each engine, and despite the very large increase in heating surface provided by the 62-element 'E' type, the total average superheat temperatures were 584°F for the 'E' type and 553°F for the Robinson. The maximum temperatures recorded were 650 and 595°F respectively. It was considered that the comparatively small increase in superheat was obtained because the superheating surface in the 'E' type was not concentrated in so effective part of the boiler as

The first 'P1' engine No 2393

The second 'P1', No 2394, fitted with 62-element 'E' type superheater

Engine No. 2562 *Isinglass* photographed during the period when she had the 62-element 'E' type super-heater—distinguishable from the double snifting valves. The engine is working a down Leeds express near Potters Bar

'P1' class engine No. 2394, with standard boiler, on heavy coal train passing Potters Bar

THE GRESLEY PACIFICS

The first 'P1' engine No 2393, as subsequently fitted with the Westinghouse brake, on up coal train near Potters Bar

that of the Robinson apparatus. No further experiments were made with the 'E' type after the successful introduction of the 43-element superheaters of the Robinson type on the 'A3' class engines. A further illustration shows No 2394 running with a standard type superheater. It is interesting to recall that O. V. S. Bulleid always regarded the 'P1' 2—8—2s as the best-looking engines Gresley ever built.

CHAPTER 5

VALVE IMPROVEMENTS AND HIGHER PRESSURES

Although the sequel to the 'Pacific' engine trials of 1923 was followed by the ordering of forty further locomotives of the Gresley type for general service on the LNER this was not the prelude to the rapid infusion of other Great Northern designs over the entire system. This book is primarily concerned with the 'Pacifics' but at the same time the general locomotive position must be briefly outlined so that the train of events from 1925 onwards may be more fully appreciated. There were two good reasons why no rapid standardisation of the entire locomotive stock was attempted. First of all money became extremely tight. After grouping, the rich and prosperous North Eastern was merged not only with its less affluent, yet comfortably solvent partners to the south and south-east, but with the Scottish companies the finances of which had been put on a shoe-string by the national agreements on railwaymen's wages. Then above all there was the chronic

incubus of the Great Central—a dead loss so far as its financial contribution to the group was concerned. So, little money was available for new locomotives.

On the second factor however, Gresley was fortunate. The motive power studs of the constituent companies were all in good shape, and once the provision for heavy main line power had been made, by the addition of the forty 'Pacifics' 2543–2582, the rest were in a good position to carry on. It was Gresley's method of dealing with this situation that built up the conditions under which the Pacifics themselves were developed. As chief mechanical engineer he had to take charge of four main works, in addition to his own at Doncaster; and no student of pre-grouping locomotive practice needs to be told that Stratford, Gorton, Darlington and Eastfield all had proudly cherished traditions of their own. Gresley, as the wise administrator he was, realised that to impose

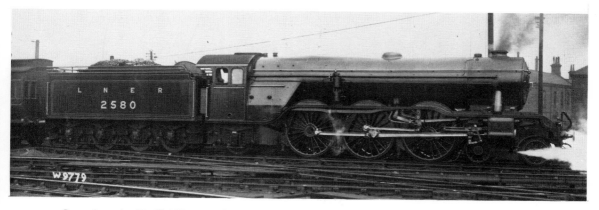

General service 'Pacific' No 2580, later named *Shotover*, in original condition, showing Westinghouse brake

67

his own Doncaster traditions on such establishments would be asking for trouble. As an old Crewe man he was probably all too well aware of what 'Midlandisation' was costing the LMS! But while allowing each major centre to carry on in its own way he made provision for a degree of central co-ordination by selecting a small personal staff, and so as to observe strict neutrality, as it were, transferring his headquarters from Doncaster to Kings Cross. On the technical side he had no more than three assistants; of these O. V. S. Bulleid was the senior, with the title of Assistant to the chief mechanical engineer. The other two were B. Spencer, for locomotives, and N. Newsome, for carriages and wagons. It was on Spencer's drawing board that most of the subsequent developments in locomotive practice took their first shape.

I must now take up the 'Pacific' story in 1925. The situation with the various main works had to be handled with some delicacy, and partly due to the personality of Bulleid there was occasional friction with Doncaster. Matters were not exactly pressed over the modified valve gear that Wintour was developing, though when this was fitted to engine No 4477 *Gay Crusader* and some indicator trials were run,

the results seemed promising. The principal consideration in working out this new layout was that there should be a minimum of alteration to the various members. New valves with $1\frac{5}{8}$ in lap were fitted, but the valve travel was increased by no more than $\frac{3}{8}$ in, to a maximum of $4\frac{15}{16}$ in and practically the only change needed to the links was a shortening of the lower arm of the combination lever. As altered *Gay Crusader* proved a free-running engine, though to an observer from the train no more so than the original 'Pacifics' at their best. She was stationed at Doncaster, and whether her drivers altered their traditional methods of working with long cut-offs and a partial opening of the regulator I cannot say. Mr Cecil J. Allen logged a run with her on the 4 pm from Kings Cross with a 16-coach train of 530 tons gross, on which the start out to Hatfield was poor, with speed falling to 36 mph on the long 1 in 200 from Wood Green to Potters Bar. But after taking $45\frac{3}{4}$ min to pass Hitchin there was some fast running, and the remaining $44\frac{1}{2}$ miles to Peterborough took exactly 40 min pass to stop. This train, in deference to its heavy load, was allowed 88 min to Peterborough and the arrival was thus $2\frac{1}{4}$ min early.

In the meantime Bert Spencer schemed out a

Engine No 2555 *Centenary*: first 'Pacific' to have the standard arrangement of long-travel valves (note casing above running plate, outboard of the outside steam pipe)

TABLES OF VALVE SETTING (FORWARD GEAR)

For Gresley 'A1' Pacifics with three 20 in × 26 in cylinders and 8 in piston-valves, original setting [lead 3/16 in, steam lap 1½ in, exhaust lap −¼ in (negative)]

Cylinder	Nominal cut-off per cent	Valve opening in		Cut-off per cent		Exhaust opens per cent		Exhaust port opening above full port in		Exhaust closes per cent	
		F	B	F	B	F	B	F	B	F	B
Outside	25	19/64	19/64	25.9	24	63.4	60.8	1/16	1/16	75.5	77
Centre	25	5/16	5/16	25.9	24.3	64.9	59.9	1/16	1/16	75.7	79.4
Outside	65	31/32	1	67	62.9	85.7	83.3	25/23	23/32	90.8	92.3
Centre	65	29/32	1	64.2	62.2	87	85		21/32	92.3	92.7
Later standard setting [lead ⅛ in, steam lap 1⅝ in, exhaust lap = line and line]											
Outside	15	12/64	13/64	14.4	15.6	65.6	65.1	5/64	4/64	65.1	65.6
Inside	15	12/64	14/64	15.3	16.5	65.9	65.3	6/64	4/64	65.3	65.9
Outisde	25	19/64	20/64	24.3	25.9	72.8	71.6	12/64	11/64	71.6	72.8
Inside	25	18/64	23/14	24.7	25.7	73	71.1	15/64	10/64	71.1	73
Outside	65	1 3/16	1 1/4	67.3	63.9	89.9	88.2	1 1/8	1 1/16	88.2	89.9
Inside	65	1 1/8	1 5/16	64.9	63.7	90.6	89.9	1 3/16	1	89.9	90.6

more complete re-design of the valve gear. At first Gresley showed little interest. One can be fairly sure that much of the time he had available for new design work, and Bulleid's too, was devoted to the 'hush-hush' four-cylinder compound 4—6—4 with the Yarrow water-tube boiler working at a pressure of 450 lb per sq in. Nearly three years were spent on the design of that boiler! So far as the 'Pacifics' were concerned, at length in response to Spencer's persistence, he agreed to have one of them fitted up with the altered valve gear. The engine concerned was 2555 *Centenary*, stationed at Doncaster, and thus conveniently based for trials afterwards. The vital statistics of the new arrangement were 5¾ in travel in full gear, 1⅝ in steam lap, lead ⅛ in, exhaust lap 'line and line'. The mechanical changes involved keeping the lower arm of the combination lever at its original length, and lengthening the shorter upper arm. This would have brought the top end above the level of the running plate, and so a raised casing was fitted, out-board of the outside steam pipe; and this minor difference in appearance henceforth made an engine with the altered valve gear easily recognisable from the earlier version. The accompanying table gives complete details of the original and modified setting of the 'Pacific' valve gear. The main points to be noticed are larger exhaust openings

in 25 per cent cut-off, and the principal feature of having good valve events at 15 per cent cut-off.

Trials were run from Doncaster on the 10.51 am up express to London, and the 4 pm down, between the modified engine, and a standard 'Pacific', No 2559. These showed that the altered gear reduced the coal consumption on this particular round trip from around 50 lb per mile to a little under 40 lb and with a sense of triumph Spencer laid the results before Gresley. There is no doubt that the Interchange Trials of 1925 had left him less impressed with the Great Western engine than many of his staff had been. In the running between Kings Cross and Doncaster the difference in coal consumption between *Pendennis Castle*, and a 'Pacific' generally acknowledged to be somewhat below top form, had not been very great, and in the early months of 1927 there were no signs of a break in the agreement on minimum times between London and Scotland. The 'Pacifics' had come through the trying period of the 1926 coal shortage better than their Great Western rivals, and having received the results of the 2555 *versus* 2559 trials he put them on one side. At that time proposals were in hand for building, experimentally, some boilers for Pacific engines with a pressure of 220 lb per sq in and Spencer felt that his modified valve gear project had been shelved. Then one day Gresley called

THE GRESLEY PACIFICS

Spencer into his office and said: 'I'm very pleased with that engine. Have the whole lot altered.' Without saying a word to any of his personal staff Gresley had sought out the workings of No 2555, made a trip on her footplate, and formed his own conclusions.

Quite apart from the very important matter of coal consumption, the outstanding point about the modified engines was that henceforth they could be driven in perfect 'copybook' style. In the many thousands of miles I have ridden on their footplates there were no more than a few isolated occasions when they were not driven with a full open regulator, and a relatively short cut-off. Working thus they had a beautifully smooth action, and the continuous roar that characterised their progress when working hard became a thing of the past. During the summer of 1927 there were not many of them about. The modified valve gear was fitted only when locomotives went into the shops for overhaul, and when the competition in length of non-stop run with the LMS began in the summer service of 1927, the Newcastle non-stop of the 9.50 am relief 'Scotsman' was worked by engines having the original standard gear. Nos 4474 and 4475 were most frequently on the job. From the locomotive point of view it was a very easy turn. For the most part the load was about 350 tons, and the average speed between Kings Cross and Newcastle only 48.7 mph. At the busiest weekends just before and just after the August Bank Holiday the load went up to 450 and 490 tons. The hardest work was required between Kings Cross and Grantham, where a start-to-pass average speed of 50 mph was scheduled; but even with a 500-ton load one would not expect the overall coal consumption to exceed 50 lb per mile, or a total of 6 tons for the trip. On the great majority of occasions it would have been much less.

My first trip with *Centenary* was indeed an eye-opener. I was interested to find her on the 1.30 pm down one afternoon when I was travelling to Peterborough. With a load of 510 tons she was not unduly hurried out to Potters Bar, taking 21 min 5 sec for this 12.7 miles, but a novel feature at once was the quietness of the exhaust, and the impression of easy working. It was in fact a little too easy to keep the initial point-to-point times, and on passing Hitchin in 40 min 55 sec we were nearly 2 min down. But by then we were really flying. Speed rose to 83½ mph at Three Counties, averaged 71 mph from Hitchin to Huntingdon, and with a brisk finish we clocked into Peterborough in exactly 81 min, 2 min early. It was an exhilarating introduction to the modified engines, but as it turned out, a mere nothing to what I was to log in the next few years.

The next important event of 1927 was signalised early in July when engine No 4480 *Enterprise* was out-shopped from Doncaster with a new boiler, carrying a pressure of 220 lb per sq in. At the time this was immediately construed as another LNER move towards Great Western practice, though it was not made without preparations for the most extensive trials. With any locomotive class of any size, and in such widespread use as the Gresley

Engine No 4480 *Enterprise*, first 'Pacific' to have 220 lb boiler and 43-element Robinson superheater

The high-pressure engine No 4480 *Enterprise* on down Leeds express near Hadley Wood

'Pacifics' it was necessary to have a number of spare boilers. At times of general repair the boiler usually takes considerably longer than the 'engine', and to keep a locomotive out of traffic for the minimum time it nearly always emerged from works after general overhaul with a different boiler from that it carried when going in. In 1927 Gresley took the opportunity to construct some of these spare boilers to carry higher pressure. This was done to obtain comparative costs of maintenance, and also to secure data as to the life of stays, and tubes, as well as the fireboxes on boilers carrying 220 lb per sq in and the standard 180 lb. The move created

much interest, because this was the first time in its history that the Doncaster Plant had constructed boilers for a higher pressure than 180 lb per sq in.

The new boilers, of which the first was put on to engine No 4480, were not just a straight copy of the original, with the necessary strengthening to sustain higher working pressure. Following his belief in high-degree superheating, the new boilers were equipped with a 43-element apparatus. This necessitated a re-arrangement of the tubes and the comparative proportions of the two boilers, both using an identical size of barrel were as follows:

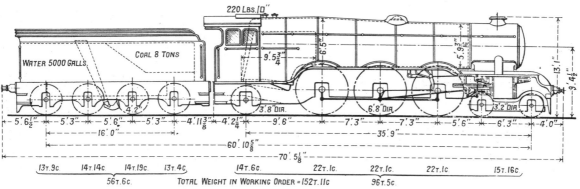

Diagram of engine No 4480 as rebuilt with 220 lb boiler

The second 220 lb engine No 2544 *Lemberg* with cylinders lined up to 18¼ in diameter

PACIFIC BOILERS		
Pressure, lb per sq in	180	220
Heating surface, sq ft		
Tubes	2715	2477
Firebox	215	215
Total evaporation	2930	2692
Superheater:		
elements	32	43
heating surface	525	703
Combined ,,	3455	3398

The tube sizes were kept the same, but the high pressure boiler had 121 small tubes of 2¼ in outside diameter, against the 168 of the 180 lb engines. The heavier boiler plates and larger superheater increased the total weight of the locomotive by 3.8 tons, and the accompanying line diagram shows how this was distributed. It was fortunate that by then the civil engineer was prepared to accept an axle load of 22 tons, and advantage was taken of this to give the modified locomotives an adhesion weight of 66 tons 3 cwt. This was not quite in proportion to the step-up in nominal tractive effort, by use of

Lemberg and *Enterprise* together at Doncaster

the higher pressure, from 29,835 to 36,465 lb; but the factor of adhesion was not reduced below four. *Enterprise* narrowly missed the chance to claim the highest tractive effort of any British passenger locomotive, because her emergence from Doncaster in rebuilt form was preceded by only a few weeks by the *King George V* from Swindon. An outward distinguishing mark of the high pressure boilers, or more correctly the boilers with the 43-element superheaters, were the square raised pads on each side of the upper part of the smokebox; as the cross-sectional drawing on page 71 shows, this covers holes that had to be cut in the smokebox to accommodate the outer ends of the superheater header.

Like other experimental versions of the Gresley 'Pacifics' *Enterprise* was stationed at Doncaster and so readily available for observation by the drawing office and works staff. Late in 1927 also, three of the North Eastern Area engines 2573 *Harvester*, 2578 *Bayardo* and 2580 *Shotover* received 220 lb boilers, also retaining their 20 in cylinders. In traffic *Enterprise* proved a highly successful engine doing most of her work on 15 per cent cut-off, and rarely needing all the regulator, except on the heaviest gradients. But by that time East Coast loads had fallen considerably from those customary in the earliest days of the 'Pacifics'. On the down road the day Leeds expresses were loading to totals of 450 and 470 tons for most of the week, and the sharply-timed 8.40 am up from Doncaster, with 111 min for the 105.5 miles from Grantham to Kings Cross, non-stop, carried a load of little more than 300 tons. For ordinary run-of-the-mill duties *Enterprise* was really too powerful, and to compare the merits of 180 and 220 lb boilers on relatively equal terms another Doncaster-based 'Pacific' was rebuilt, No 2544 *Lemberg*, but with cylinders lined up to $18\frac{1}{4}$ in. This provided a 220 lb engine with almost exactly the same tractive effort as the 180 lb engines.

The year 1927 was one of intense rivalry between the locomotive departments of the four British main line railways. The Southern was busy running indicator trials with the *Lord Nelson*, briefly, the most powerful express locomotive in the country; the praises of the Great Western 'Kings' were being loudly sung on both sides of the Atlantic; and in the late autumn the LMS was running dynamometer car trials to show what powerful and efficient engines they now had in the new 'Royal Scots'. In February 1928 there took place the classic series of trials on the LNER between a standard 180 lb 'Pacific', newly fitted with long travel

The 180 lb engine in the 1927 trials: No. 4473 *Solario* with long-travel valves on down Leeds express near New Barnet

COMPARATIVE TESTS OF LOCOMOTIVES WITH 180 AND 220 LB. PRESSURE

TABLE I.—Dynamometer Car Tests, L.N.E.R. "Pacific" Engine No. 4473, Pressure 180 lb.

Road	Trip 1	Trip 2	Trip 3	Trip 4	Trip 5	Trip 6
	Doncaster to King's Cross and return.	Doncaster to King's Cross and return.	Doncaster to King's Cross and return.	Doncaster to King's Cross and return.	Doncaster to King's Cross and return.	Doncaster to King's Cross and return.
Date	13-2-28	14-2-28	15-2-28	16-2-28	17-2-28	18-2-28
Trip	1	2	3	4	5	6
Weight behind tender, tons	(a) 427·0 (b) 495·25 (c) 334·25	(a) 430·5 (b) 495·75 (c) 327·75	(a) 425·5 (b) 494·25 (c) 333·25	(a) 439·75 (b) 488·75 (c) 331·75	(a) 432·25 (b) 488·25 (c) 332·25	(a) 456·25 (b) 489·75 (c) 333·75
Total weight of train including engine, tons	(a) 567·0 (b) 635·25 (c) 474·25	(a) 570·5 (b) 635·75 (c) 467·75	(a) 565·5 (b) 634·25 (c) 473·25	(a) 579·75 (b) 628·75 (c) 471·25	(a) 572·25 (b) 628·25 (c) 472·25	(a) 596·25 (b) 629·75 (c) 473·75
Coal per mile, lb.	40·1	34·95	37·93	40·65	40·61	38·76
Coal per D.B.H.P. hour, lb.	3·44	3·09	2·89	2·99	3·06	3·00
Coal per ton-mile, lb.	0·072	0·062	0·068	0·072	0·072	0·068
Coal per sq. ft. of grate area per hour, lb.	50·43	44·13	47·73	51·63	52·82	51·0
Water, lb. per lb. of coal, lb.	7·97	8·11	8·3	8·46	7·95	8·3
Water per D.B.H.P. hour, lb.	26·9 / 27·9	24·7 / 25·4	23·8 / 24·2	24·3 / 26·4	23·8 / 24·9	24·4 / 25·5
Gallons per mile	31·65 / 32·2	27·9 / 28·75	30·5 / 32·5	33·7 / 35·0	31·6 / 32·8	31·8 / 32·5
Average speed, m.p.h.	49·2 / 54·9	49·7 / 54·8	50·65 / 53·3	50·22 / 54·83	51·6 / 56·08	53·0 / 55·7
Work done in H.P. hours	1766·8 / 1867·0	1712·6 / 1816·0	1958·5 / 2125·3	2070·3 / 2164·6	2059·6 / 2078·1	1987·5 / 2034·6

NOTE.—Coal per ton-mile includes weight of engine, but excludes coal used for shed duties. Rossington coal used throughout. Boiler pressure 180 lb. per square inch.
(a) Doncaster to King's Cross and return. (b) King's Cross to Peterborough; (c) Peterborough to Doncaster.

TABLE II.—Dynamometer Car Tests, L.N.E.R. "Pacific" Engine No. 2544, Pressure 220 lb.

Road	Trip 1	Trip 2	Trip 3	Trip 4	Trip 5
	Doncaster to King's Cross and return.	Doncaster to King's Cross and return.	Doncaster to King's Cross and return.	Doncaster to King's Cross and return.	Doncaster to King's Cross and return.
Date	20-2-28	21-2-28	22-2-28	23-2-28	24-2-28
Trip	1	2	3	4	5
Weight behind tender, tons	(a) 433·75 (b) 506·75 (c) 348·75	(a) 428·75 (b) 508·25 (c) 347·25	(a) 424·75 (b) 505·75 (c) 346·75	(a) 427·75 (b) 502·25 (c) 346·25	(a) 428·75 (b) 512·25 (c) 355·25
Total weight of train including engine, tons	(a) 577·75 (b) 650·75 (c) 492·75	(a) 572·75 (b) 652·25 (c) 491·25	(a) 568·75 (b) 649·75 (c) 490·75	(a) 571·75 (b) 646·25 (c) 490·25	(a) 572·75 (b) 656·25 (c) 490·25
Coal per mile, lb.	37·18	35·89	35·4	34·39	34·01
Coal per D.B.H.P. hour, lb.	3·27	3·17	3·24	2·92	2·99
Coal per ton-mile, lb.	0·065	0·063	0·062	0·060	0·059
Coal per sq. ft. of grate area per hour, lb.	49·6	47·92	46·8	45·4	44·32
Water, lb. per lb. of coal, lb.	7·67	7·82	8·32	8·75	8·31
Water per D.B.H.P. hour, lb.	24·35 / 25·81	24·18 / 25·51	25·53 / 28·52	25·15 / 28·76	23·9 / 25·76
Gallons per mile	28·7 / 28·3	28·9 / 27·18	28·58 / 30·38	31·42 / 30·38	27·22 / 29·28
Average speed, m.p.h.	58·3 / 52·16	57·18 / 53·3	57·5 / 51·8	55·55 / 53·5	55·7 / 51·93
Work done in H.P. hours	1837·0 / 1709·8	1862·8 / 1658·5	1745·5 / 1660·7	1947·6 / 1729·3	1775·1 / 1773·8

NOTE.—Coal per ton-mile includes weight of engine, but excludes coal used for shed duties. Rossington coal used throughout. Boiler pressure 220 lb. per square inch.
(a) Doncaster to King's Cross. (b) King's Cross to Peterborough. (c) Peterborough to Doncaster.

valves, No 4473 *Solario*, and the high pressure engine No 2544 *Lemberg*. As in the case of earlier dynamometer car trials the up runs were made on the Leeds express due into Kings Cross at 1.55 pm, but with *Solario* and *Lemberg* the normal return working was used, by the 4 pm down, which was then considerably faster than in 1923, and which with its daily loads of over 500 tons tare to Peterborough provided an excellent test of capacity.

As usual the locomotives were worked by Doncaster men. Coal was weighed on to the tenders and off after each day's running. Coal for lighting up and for use until each engine was on its train was weighed separately and not included in the figures given in the accompanying tables. The tenders were calibrated and the water was carefully measured by a suitable indicator. The trials began on 13 February, with engine No 4473, which made six round trips between Doncaster and Kings Cross. The comparative series with No 2544 were carried out in the following week. The weather during the trials with engine No 4473 was not so favourable as during the week of No 2544's tests. In consequence the former engine exerted a little more horsepower in running the trains to time. But although the measurement of coal

and water consumption in relation to the total work done can be considered to compensate in some ways for the variables inevitably connected with dynamometer car test runs on service trains, the experience of testing in more recent years has shown how extraneous circumstances can affect the seemingly basic performance characteristics of a steam locomotive.

If one studies the summary of the tests set out in the table (opposite), it is seen that the coal consumption per dbhp hour of engine No 4473 varied between 2.89 and 3.44 lb—a 19 per cent increase of maximum over minimum; and almost as big disparities can be seen if one compares runs when the coal consumption was just over 40 lb a mile, as on trips 1 and 4. But taken all round there was a remarkable consistency of performance between the two locomotives, and the averages of 3.08 lb per dbhp hour (No 4473) and 3.12 (No 2544) show thermal efficiencies that even the Great Western would have found hard to surpass. The report does not quote the calorific value of the Rossington coal used throughout the tests, but it is lower than that of the Welsh coal with which *Caldicot Castle* achieved the results published by Mr Collett at the World Power Conference in 1924. The most direct comparison that can

Long travel valves becoming standard: engine No 2557 *Blair Athol* so equipped on down express near Potters Bar

THE GRESLEY PACIFICS

Up East Coast express leaving York: engine No. 2568 *Sceptre*

be made with the published coal consumption in the Interchange Trials of 1925 is that of coal per train mile. Although the train loads in 1928 were on the whole lighter, averaging around 430 tons tare in the up direction, 500 down from Kings Cross to Peterborough and 340 onwards to Doncaster, there is all the difference in the world between the consistent returns of over 50 lb per mile by *both* competitors, in 1925, and the averages of 38.83 lb per mile by No 4473 and the even more remarkable 35.37 lb by No 2544. The details of each individual round trip, given in the table shown on page 74 provide a most fascinating study, and show clearly that Gresley and his staff had, by 1928, developed the original GNR 'Pacific' into a truly outstanding locomotive.

In a leading article commenting on these test results *The Engineer* was moved to write:

In reviewing generally the present trend of development, one fact becomes apparent. It is the great and far-reaching improvements which are continually being made in the design of the steam locomotive, which result in better performance and which, without doubt, strengthen its already strong position as still the most effective and commercially efficient means of providing railway motive power. There are certain definite reasons for the improvements which are manifest in recent construction. In the first place, much more is now known of the principles on which boiler design and proportions are founded, and in many other respects the work carried out on testing plants has broadened our knowledge [this was clearly referring to current Pennsylvania work on the Altoona plant] and, secondly, what is more important, designers are making use of the information now available, so that locomotives of comparative simple construction designed and built, with the elements essential to success kept well in view, are giving working results hardly thought of but a few years ago. In spite of this notable progress, however, we do not hesitate to say that the development of the steam locomotive is far from complete. Avenues which give promise of providing opportunities for further improvement still remain to be explored. There are, for example, already well marked indications that valve gear changes which will influence for the better cylinder performance to at least as great an extent as that attained by the use of the long lap as against the short lap slide valves, are taking place. As an indication of what can be accomplished with a simple expansion locomotive of normal design, the fuel consumption figures given by Mr Gresley are of exceptional interest. He has, as is well known, rebuilt some of his 'Pacifics' with boilers having a higher steam pressure than has been his usual practice. The pressure adopted is

220 lb as against 180 lb previously employed, and further opportunity was taken to increase the size of the superheater, which is larger by some 34 per cent. Trials carried out between Kings Cross and Doncaster have given some astonishing results . . .

Then after quoting the overall figures already mentioned, *The Engineer* concludes:

It is an interesting fact that the coal per drawbar horsepower was lower for the 180 lb engine than for the 220 lb. On the other hand the speed attained by the high pressure engine was on the whole greater than that of the low. It must, however, be observed that the former was favoured by better weather. Making due allowance for good coal and expert handling the figures for both engines, and more especially—as far as coal per ton mile is concerned—for that having the higher steam pressure, are excellent, and, indeed, are *better than any* which have so far come to our knowledge.

The figures quoted for coal per ton mile in the tables includes the weight of the locomotive in the load. If these are adjusted to relate only to the trailing load the figures become 0.093 lb for No 4473 and 0.084 lb for the No 2544. *The Engineer* was certainly justified in its claim for supremacy on this basis, for the corresponding figure for *Caldicot Castle* in the 1924 dynamometer car trials between Swindon and Plymouth was 0.101 lb—a most significant advantage to the LNER. Gresley and his staff had every reason to be gratified by these results, which

were, in no small measure, due to Spencer's activities. The stigma of 'defeat' in the Interchange Trials of 1925 had been most triumphantly wiped out.

As in the dynamometer car trials of 1928, so in ordinary service, one could not detect a great deal of difference between the work of the 180 lb and 220 lb engines—the former, that is, which had been fitted with long travel valves. Moreover to the casual observer the unaltered engines were still putting up very good performances, though as we now know at a cost in coal consumption that would have been quite unacceptable in the conditions of accelerated service that was required from 1932 onwards. One of the last runs I had with one of the unaltered engines was on the 10.10 am down from Kings Cross, with a gross trailing load of 485 tons and engine No 4471 *Sir Frederick Banbury*. It was a very rough winter's day, and although we made an excellent start out of Kings Cross, passing Finsbury Park in 6½ min, speed fell away to 36 mph on the ascent to Potters Bar and we took 26 min 35 sec to pass Hatfield. Then however the engine ran as freely as *Centenary* had done on my first trip with one of the altered engines, touching 83½ mph at Three Counties, taking only 22¾ min for the 27 miles from Hitchin to Huntingdon, and clocking in to Peterborough in 80 min 25 sec, 2½ min early.

Some weeks later I was on the 1.30 pm from Kings Cross with one of the altered engines, No 2559 *The Tetrarch*, which in its original form

Up Newcastle express on Ganwick curve: engine No 2550 *Blink Bonny*

THE GRESLEY PACIFICS

LNER 1.30 PM KINGS CROSS—DONCASTER

Load: 505 tons tare, 545 tons full
Engine: 4—6—2 No 2559 *The Tetrarch*

Dist miles		Sch min	Actual m	Actual s	Speeds mph
0.0	KINGS CROSS .	0	0	00	—
2.6	Finsbury Park .		6	40	—
5.0	Wood Green .		9	50	55½
9.2	New Barnet .		15	05	46½
12.7	Potters Bar .		19	55	43
17.7	HATFIELD .	25	25	00	72
23.5	*Woolmer Green* .		30	30	55½
26.7	*Langley Jc* .		33	35	69
28.6	Stevenage .		35	20	64½
31.9	HITCHIN .	39	38	10	77½
35.7	Three Counties .		41	00	80½
41.1	Biggleswade .		45	20	72/75
51.7	St Neots .		54	55	57
58.9	HUNTINGDON .	64	61	45	66 (max)
62.0	*Milepost 62* .		65	30	43
69.4	Holme .		72	40	75
75.0	*Fletton Jc* .		78	10	—
76.4	PETERBOROUGH	83	80	15	
3.1	*Werrington Jc* .		6	05	55½
8.4	Tallington .		11	30	64½
12.2	Essendine .		15	10	61½
20.7	Corby .		24	45	46/52½
23.7	*Stoke Box* .		28	25	48
29.1	GRANTHAM .	35	33	45	69/53
—			sigs.		
43.7	NEWARK .		48	40	45
51.0	Crow Park .		56	15	64½
57.3	*Markham Box* .		63	05	50
62.2	RETFORD .		67	40	75
67.5	Ranskill .		72	25	66½
73.1	*Milepost 149½* .		77	50	53
76.8	*Black Carr Jc* .		81	20	69
79.6	DONCASTER .	88	85	15	

was tested against No 2555 in 1927, and we had a sixteen-coach train of 545 gross trailing tons. This splendid performance is worth full tabulation, and points to be specially noted are the fine ascent from Wood Green, with a time of less than 20 min through Potters Bar, and the fast running over the undulations from Hatfield, which took us through Hitchin nearly a minute *early*. Although the engine was obviously quite capable of it there was no need for undue haste afterwards and from Biggleswade onwards it looked like 'killing time'! From Hitchin to Fletton Junction the time was 1¾ min longer than on the run with 4471 on the 10.10 am mentioned previously.

I was travelling through to Leeds on this occasion, and as the tabulated details show we continued in first class style throughout. The start out of Peterborough with this massive train was particularly good. I have seen it suggested that because of the limitation of cut-off in full gear to 65 per cent that the Gresley 'Pacifics' as a class were poor starters, particularly where there are sharp gradients, or curves to be negotiated from the platform ends. But there could not be much the matter with an engine that could lift a 545-ton train off the mark, on a rising gradient of 1 in 270 for three-quarters of a mile, and have it skimming along on the level at 55½ mph in just over 3 miles from rest! From Werrington Junction the 20.6 miles up to Stoke summit took only 22 min 20 sec, and after passing Grantham it was again a case of killing time until the slight signal check at Newark. Then to make sure of things a splendid concluding effort was made, climbing to Markham at no lower speed than 50 mph and covering the 17.7 miles from Gamston Box to Black Carr Junction at an average speed of 65 mph. This was an excellent example of what we would regard as top class performance on the Great Northern section of the LNER prior to the accelerations of 1932.

I logged another good run in the same period with one of the Grantham engines, No 4479 *Robert the Devil* on the 7.25 pm night Highland express, allowed 121 min for the 105 miles nonstop run to Grantham. The load was 560 gross trailing tons, and although the engine was justifiably driven somewhat easier on the banks, the running as far as Peterborough was right up to schedule requirements of the fastest Leeds trains. A slight check near Welwyn North lengthened our time out to Hitchin to 41 min 35 sec, but then we continued in what was then becoming characteristic style. Maximum speed below Hitchin was 79 mph; the 27 miles on to Huntingdon took 22¾ min, and Peterborough was passed in 82 min 25 sec. The engine was not unduly pressed on the climb to Stoke, taking 24 min 25 sec for the 20.6 miles from Werrington and Grantham was reached 1¾ min early—119 min 15 sec from Kings Cross.

CHAPTER 6

THE EDINBURGH NON-STOPS

The summer of 1927 showed that the LMS had got the 'bit' of publicity fairly between their teeth. The morning Anglo-Scottish express service, newly named 'The Royal Scot', may have been a poor job from the locomotive point of view, double-headed throughout, but it was first rate publicity and the Newcastle non-stop of the LNER, made in one direction only, attracted little comparable attention, even though it was the longer run. Then with the winter service of 1927–8 the LMS pushed things a big step further. The new 3-cylinder 4—6—0s of the 'Royal Scot' class were coming into service, and the venturesome project was launched of running the 10 am down from Euston, and the 10 am up from Glasgow non-stop in each direction between Euston and Carlisle, 299.2 miles, with a 440-ton train single-headed throughout with one of the new engines. A highly competitive situation was

thus set up. The daily record length of non-stop run so long held by the Cornish Riviera Express, was left far behind, and the LMS was holding not only the British, but the world record for length of non-stop run—a remarkable situation when one compares the size of our country with some others in the world.

During the winter of 1927–8, when the LMS were demonstrating that their ambitious timing could be kept with reliability during the season of inclement weather, railway enthusiasts and many others too were wondering how the LNER would reply. Gresley was not the man to take such a challenge lying down, but still the old 'gentleman's' agreement on minimum times to the Scottish cities prevailed. There was direct competition for the London–Edinburgh traffic. The winter formation of the new 'Royal Scot' express included a six-coach portion, with its own dining and kitchen car for Edinburgh,

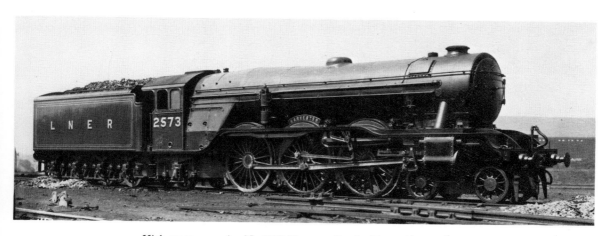

High pressure engine No 2573 *Harvester* fitted with corridor tender

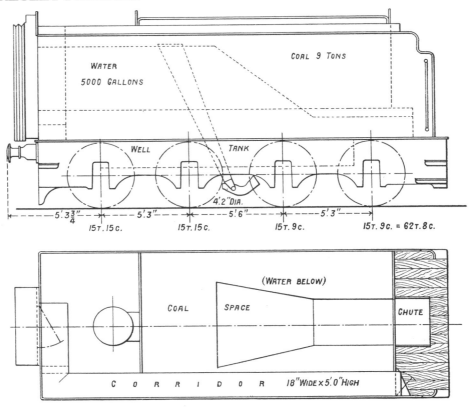

WATER
5000 GALLONS

COAL 9 TONS

WELL   TANK

4'2"DIA.

5'3¾"   5'3"   5'6"   5'3"

15T. 15 C.   15T. 15 C.   15T. 9 C.   15T. 9 C. = 62T. 8 C.

(WATER BELOW)

COAL   SPACE   CHUTE

C O R R I D O R   18" WIDE x 5'0" HIGH

Elevation and plan of corridor tender

where the arrival time was 6.15 pm. So far as length of non-stop run was concerned, if the LNER was out to recapture the record in the summer of 1928 it would mean running through to Berwick at least, and it was in this atmosphere that the idea of the Edinburgh non-stop was

View from rear of No 2573 showing the corridor tender connection

80

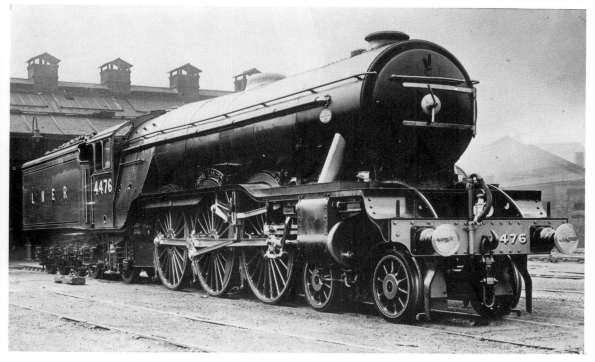

One of the two original London engines fitted with corridor tender No. 4476 *Royal Lancer*

conceived. Mrs Violet Godfrey, one of Gresley's daughters, has told the amusing story of how she went into the dining room of their home one evening and found her father with a line of chairs, backs to the wall, making his way carefully along between those 'backs' and the wall. Laughingly she asked whatever he was doing. Gresley replied: 'If I can get through that space so can my drivers.' He was a tall, and powerfully built man, and by this homely experiment he was settling the principal dimension of one feature that made the Edinburgh 'non-stop' a practical proposition, namely the corridor tender.

It had been felt that the limit of the powers of a single engine crew had been reached in the Newcastle non-stop of the previous year, and that it was undesirable on grounds of safety to carry two crews on one engine, commodious though the cabs of the Gresley 'Pacifics' were. So the idea of the corridor tender was conceived. Gresley determined that a passage 18 in wide by 5 ft high would be adequate. The resulting layout of the tender is shown in the accompanying drawing, and quite apart from the corridor feature the tender was redesigned so as to carry an extra ton of coal, rather than less. It was

realised that the empty space of the corridor on one side would result in a certain lack of balance, and so some counterweighting approximately equal to the weight of water and coal that would have occupied the space of the corridor was added immediately below the corridor. With these extra provisions the new tenders weighed 62 tons 8 cwt, fully loaded, as compared with the 56.5 tons of the original standard tenders. As previously the tenders were eight-wheeled, with rigid axles.

Travelling from Leeds to Kings Cross on 10 April 1928, I saw outside the entrance to Doncaster Plant the first two 'Pacifics' to be fitted with the new tenders. These were 4472 *Flying Scotsman* and 4476 *Royal Lancer*, and I noticed that both had been equipped with the modified valve gear. They had been up to London for demonstration to the Press, and other interested parties, prior to the inauguration of non-stop running between Kings Cross and Edinburgh as early in the season as 1 May 1928. Opportunity was taken in the environs of Kings Cross to demonstrate the connections between the tender and the leading coach. The sharp curves and numerous turnouts and crossings between the engine yard at Kings Cross

THE GRESLEY PACIFICS

The first London–Edinburgh non-stop: the Lord Mayor of London, Sir Charles Batho on the footplate
with Mr Gresley and Driver A. Pibworth

and 'Top Shed' provided an excellent test; and those who witnessed it were clearly impressed with the freedom and smoothness with which the connections between tender and coach performed. A total of ten corridor tenders was built in that first year because apart from the two locomotives actually engaged on the run it was obviously essential to have others standing by.

The forthcoming inauguration of the 'non-stop', by far the longest in the world ever to be worked by a locomotive of any kind, was given immense advance publicity; and the LMS by an amusing, though quite transient gesture, stole a morsel of the LNER thunder by breaking the new 'record' five days before it had been inaugurated. On Friday 27 April 'The Royal Scot' was run in two portions, and both ran non-stop to their respective Scottish destinations 399.7 miles to Edinburgh, and 401.4 to Glasgow; but this experiment was not repeated. On 1 May 1928, the 'Flying Scotsman' set out simultaneously from Kings Cross and Edinburgh Waverley, on the first northbound and southbound non-stop runs respectively. The engine from London was No 4472 *Flying Scotsman* and

from Edinburgh it was one of those recently fitted with a high pressure boiler, No 2580 *Shotover*. It is worth recalling the names of the enginemen on those historic inaugural journeys; all were well-known to railway enthusiasts of the time. On No 4472 was A. Pibworth of Kings Cross, who had taken No 4474 to Plymouth in 1925, and Tom Blades of Gateshead, who had brought the NER 'Pacific' No 2400 to London in 1923, and had fired the 4—4—0 No 1620 on the last night of the 1895 'race'. From Edinburgh No 2580 had Tom Henderson, a mighty runner with North British 'Atlantics', and J. Day, of Kings Cross who was pilotman to W. Young on *Pendennis Castle* in the 1925 Interchange Trials.

If the advance publicity for the introduction of the new service had been strong, the public interest on 1 May was unprecedented. At Kings Cross the crowds were so great that high officers of the LNER found great difficulty in making their way to the locomotives, and the engine crews were greeted with the utmost enthusiasm. It was the same at the principal intermediate stations en route. But despite all this, those who were in the habit of making a close study of locomotive performance at the time found little cause for elation. It was pointed out that to avoid arrivals at journey's end earlier than 6.15 pm no less than 26 min *extra* running time had been added to the down train, and 31 min to the up. Others questioned why it should have been necessary to maintain the 6.15 pm arrival times, seeing that, seemingly within the terms of the 'agreement', the fastest East Coast night trains before World War 1 had been scheduled to reach Edinburgh in 7¾ hr from Kings Cross, and that schedule had been revived for a short time after the war. Others suggested that if the practical purpose of the non-stop running was to give passengers a completely undisturbed journey from London to Edinburgh it could have been done much more economically by stopping for a few moments at Clifton Junction, York, to re-man, thus saving all expense of the two crews and the complication of the corridor tender.

This last suggestion would however have defeated the whole idea of the non-stop run. It was the length of the run that 'drew the crowds' as it were. Many times when I travelled on the train and its BR successors 'The Capitals Limited' and the 'Elizabethan' I was impressed with the immense care taken to ensure that the run was actually made *non-stop*. Much of the prestige, and of the fame the service eventually gathered to itself, would have been lost, if signal stops occurred en route, even though time was made up subsequently, and the eventual arrival was punctual, or ahead of time. In this connection, despite the relatively slow overall speed it was not an altogether easy train to run. There were some close margins at certain places, notably at York and Newcastle at summer weekends; and although the greatest care was taken to give it a clear road those areas then had nought but semaphore signals controlled by a multitude of manually worked boxes. Co-ordination was not always easy, and if the non-stop had approached 4 or 5 min early there was a good chance it would have been stopped.

On the first day neither the down nor the up train was logged in detail, but the following times, taken from the journal, give a good impression of what was involved:

Dist miles				Actual time		Av speed mph
0.0	Kings Cross	.	.	10	00 am	—
76.4	Peterborough	.	.	11	24 ,,	54.5
105.5	Grantham	.	.	11	58 ,,	51.4
156.0	Doncaster	.	.	12	54 pm	54.1
188.2	York	.	.	1	37 ,,	44.9
268.3	Newcastle	.	.	3	22 ,,	45.7
335.2	Berwick	.	.	4	50 ,,	45.6
392.7	Edinburgh	.	.	6	03 ,,	47.3

The first London–Edinburgh non-stop leaving Kings Cross, 1 May 1928, engine No 4472 *Flying Scotsman*

Engine No 2547 *Doncaster*, one of the few not named after a racehorse

The train had to run relatively fast down to Grantham to keep ahead of the 'Junior Scotsman' which left Kings Cross at 10.5 am and made all the usual stops. It was an absolute 'doddle' after that, and even with such leisurely running as is revealed by the average speeds the train arrived in Edinburgh 12 min early.

The southbound train made the times shown in the adjoining table.

From these times one can appreciate why train running enthusiasts took a poor view of the new service. The tare load of the train was no more than 386 tons, though this was in-

Dist miles				Actual time		Av speed mph
0.0	Edinburgh	.	.	10	00 am	—
57.5	Berwick .	.	.	11	10 ,,	49.3
124.4	Newcastle	.	.	12	40 pm	44.6
204.5	York .	.	.	2	18 ,,	49.0
236.7	Doncaster	.	.	2	58 ,,	48.3
287.2	Grantham	.	.	4	4 ,,	45.9
392.7	Kings Cross	.	.	6	12½ ,,	49.3

creased by one or two coaches at times of the heaviest traffic; but even so, in the light of what the Gresley 'Pacifics' were doing daily on the Leeds trains between Kings Cross and Don-

One of the Haymarket 'Pacifics' No 2567 *Sir Visto*

caster it was regarded by the stop-watching fraternity as a travesty of a job.

But there was far more to this epoch-marking schedule than mere speed—or lack of it; and this brings me back to the locomotives themselves. On the inaugural trip a very experienced observer and commentator on locomotive practice, the late Charles S. Lake, then technical editor of *The Railway Gazette*, travelled in Gresley's company, and with him spent some time on the footplate. He estimated that at the end of the journey about 2 tons of coal remained on the tender. Assuming that it was fully coaled

even more apparent in much later years with the Peppercorn 'A1' class and their 50 sq ft grates. In comparable service, particularly when very heavy continuous steaming was not required, the Gresley engines with $41\frac{1}{4}$ sq ft of grate area were consistently lighter on coal, because—as a running superintendent explained to me—they had to fire coal on the bigger engines simply to keep the firebars covered. With the first class Yorkshire coal normally used on the crack East Coast trains, the normal practice was to have a thin fire spread evenly over the grate, and in conditions of light steaming, as on the non-stop

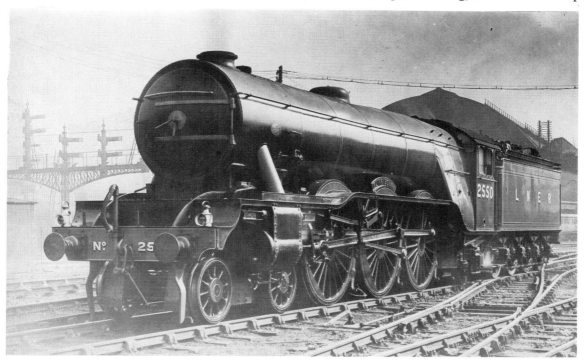

Always a Grantham engine, No 2550 *Blink Bonny* in Kings Cross locomotive yard

up with 9 tons on when leaving the shed for Kings Cross station, 7 tons had been used on the journey, or an average over the 393 miles of 40 lb per mile. In view of the coal consumption figure returned by the sister engine No 4473 *Solario* in the dynamometer car trials of February 1928 with considerably heavier and faster trains, the estimated figure for No 4472 may seem rather high, and one that left little margin for working on days of rough weather, or when traffic requirements demanded an extra one or two coaches on the train. Actually, however, No 4472 was demonstrating a characteristic of the Doncaster wide-firebox engines, which became

Flying Scotsman the coal consumption could become proportional to the grate area!

All the same, it would have become manifestly impossible to run from Kings Cross to Edinburgh non-stop with the original valve gear. An increase from 40 to 45 lb per mile would have put the total consumption up to nearly 8 tons, and reduced the practical margin to very near the minimum. In that first year of non-stop running care had to be taken to use only engines that had been fitted with long travel valves; for although this was to a large extent safeguarded by the attachment of the corridor tender, there was nothing to preclude the changing of a tender, in emergency. So far as the manning of the non-stop was concerned, it was originally shared between Kings Cross, Gateshead and Haymarket sheds, with an allocation of 4, 6, and 4 crews from each shed. In this respect it was an important step towards the complete integration of engine workings on the East Coast Route. It brought enginemen from the former Great Northern, North Eastern and North British Railways into a partnership that no interpenetration workings could have done, and helped to break down the barrier of North Eastern prejudice against the Gresley 'Pacifics'. Above all, the 'non-stop' was an outstanding daily reliability test for the engines themselves, in the efficiency of lubrication of all the moving parts, and in the continuity of the steaming.

The Gresley 'Pacifics' were apt to be regarded by some commentators as well-nigh immaculate in their steaming, with the wide shallow firebox a veritable panacea against all the hazards of indifferent coal. This, of course, was not so, and on my own first footplate journey on one of them, no farther than from Doncaster to Kings Cross an engine with a normally very good reputation went very sadly 'off the boil' south of Peterborough and involved us in considerable loss of time. While from all accounts they had a very comfortable trip on the inaugural down journey with 4472, I know it was not always so,

and I heard of cases when the fireman on the second stage of the journey was so hard pressed that the driver asked for the relief man to come through again and lend a hand. I remember well the plaintive remark of an LMS fireman when I was on the footplate on a Carlisle–Euston non-stop run: 'If only we could *stop* for two or three minutes, I'd have this fire back into shape and we could easily make up the time'! But stopping for a 'blow-up' was the last thing anyone would countenance on the 'non-stop', and on one had to go regardless.

In this connection some interesting trials were carried out on the boiler of one of the original standard 'Pacifics', No 2578 *Bayardo* to obtain the evaporative performance. They are very important as one of the very first attempts to obtain a truly scientific relation between coal consumption and steam production. Gresley was one of the foremost advocates of an up-to-date stationary plant for locomotive testing; but in the straitened economic circumstances of the early 1930s capital expenditure on such a project was out of the question, and a most ingenious improvisation with existing plant was rigged up for this series of tests. The engine, stationary at the time, had the dynamometer car coupled to the front buffer beam. All connections to the cylinders were blanked off, and a pipe leading from the outside steam pipe

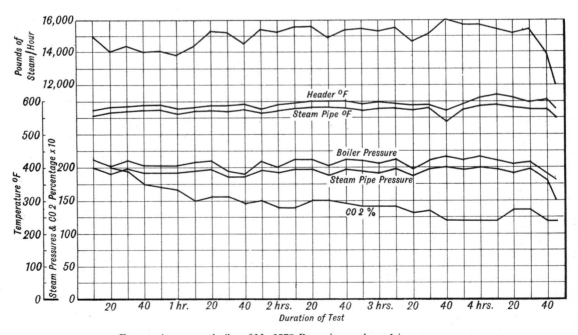

Evaporation test on boiler of No 2578 *Bayardo*: results at 1 in water gauge

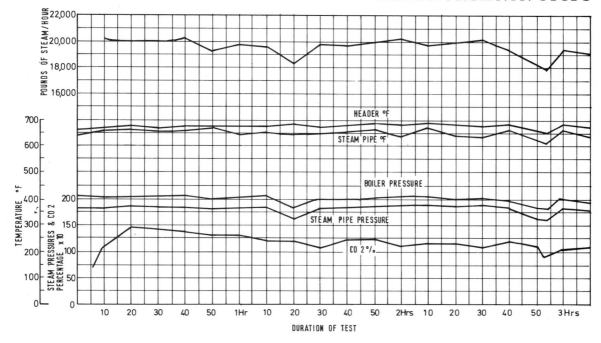

Evaporation test: results at 3 in water gauge

on the right hand side of the engine led down, and along the length of the dynamometer car. In this special pipe were fitted instruments for measuring temperature and pressure of the steam, and further along the pipe an orifice-type flow meter was installed. Beyond this meter was a branch forming a return path for the steam, taken to the side of the blast pipe which was blanked off from the cylinders. The necessary dials and recording instruments were arranged inside the dynamometer car.

Just as trials at constant steam rate were carried out on a number of locomotives in British Railways days, at both Swindon and Rugby, so this Gresley 'Pacific' was steamed at various constant rates of evaporation, and became in fact the first British locomotive ever to be subjected to such tests. Three separate tests were carried out, the first with smokebox vacuum at 1 in of water, and a rate of evaporation averaging 15,000 lb of steam per hr. In recent years this would be regarded as fairly light working. This test was continued for $4\frac{3}{4}$ hr, and the results are shown in the accompanying graphs. The coal, from Wylam Colliery, had a calorific value of 13,772 BThU per lb. The firing rate was 1886 lb per hr equal to 31.4 lb per mile at 50 mph. Related to the grate, it was

only 45.7 lb per sq ft of grate per hr, whereas in the 1928 trials between Doncaster and Kings Cross the competing engines 4473 and 2544 were showing figures varying between 44 and 53 lb per sq ft of grate area per hr. A steam rate of 15,000 lb per hr could therefore be considered as something below the needs of the fastest express work of the day, but approximating to the demands of the 'non-stop'.

The second trial, of which the relevant graphs are also shown, was made at an average rate of evaporation of 20,000 lb per hr, which at that time was considered to be more than would be required except under very exceptional conditions. The comparative results are shown below. A further test was made to see what maximum evaporation could be obtained from the boiler; but under the 'rigged-up' test con-

BOILER PERFORMANCE: 220 LB PACIFICS		
Test No	1	2
Target evaporation lb per hr	15,000	20,000
Actual evaporation lb per hr	15,320	19,924
Duration of test	$4\frac{3}{4}$ hr	$3\frac{1}{4}$ hr
Coal consumed per hr lb	1886	2757
Coal per sq ft of grate area per hr lb	45.7	66.8
Evaporation lb of water per lb coal	8.12	7.22
Boiler efficiency per cent	78.2	71.6

THE GRESLEY PACIFICS

'The Flying Scotsman' crossing the Royal Border Bridge, Berwick-upon-Tweed: engine No 2574 *St. Frusquin* and a 14-coach load

ditions accurate measurement of all the various quantities could not be obtained, and the maximum smokebox vacuum that could be raised was $3\frac{1}{4}$ in.

At the maximum output test an evaporation of 27,360 lb per hour was secured, but the coal consumption is not quoted in the report.

These results, while having a particular bearing on the working of the non-stop 'Flying Scotsman', are also of great interest as being the only results that have ever been published of the detailed performance of the Gresley 'Pacific' boiler. Inevitably one wishes to make comparisons, and thoughts naturally turn to the Great Western 'Castles'. The following table gives some results taken from the now-famous report of Mr Collett to the World Power Conference, in 1924.

'CASTLE' AND 'PACIFIC' BOILERS

Engine	'Castle'	'Pacific'
Boiler pressure psi	225	220
Coal consumed per hr lb	1940	1886
Coal per sq ft of grate per hr lb	66.1	45.7
Evaporation per lb of coal from and at 212°F	12.2	11.1
Evaporation, actual per lb of coal	8.95	8.12
Calorific value of coal BThU per lb	14,780	13,772
Boiler efficiency per cent	79.8	78.2

In the above table one is comparing a stationary test, admittedly with a rigged-up plant, against the average figures of a road trial. It will be

seen, however, that on the above basis, if adjustment is made for the difference in calorific value of the coal there was very little in it. The actual evaporation of the 'Pacific' rises to 8.72 lb of water per lb of coal, and the difference between this and the 'Castle' figure of 8.95 lb is almost exactly reflected in the boiler efficiencies. These tests carried out on engine No 2578 *Bayardo* confirm in precise figures, what was generally considered to be the case, namely that the Gresley boiler as fitted to the 'Pacifics' was second to none among British express passenger locomotives. One interesting point emerging from the boiler tests on *Bayardo*, was that the steam temperature at the superheater header never quite reached 700°F. The maximum recorded was 680°F.

The non-stop *Flying Scotsman* retained its leisurely schedule of $8\frac{1}{4}$ hr between London and Edinburgh for four summer seasons; but in 1932 no less than 45 min were cut out, giving arrival times at each end at 5.30 pm. With the experience of four seasons running at the original times and numerous slight detail improvements in the engine design the acceleration could confidently be undertaken, and the timing of 450 min, representing an average speed of 52.4 mph, was the fastest booked while no more modern engines than the non-streamlined 'Pacifics' were available.

At the end of the summer season, after the

'non-stop' had ceased to run, some of the loco-motive workings remained as during the non-stop period with one engine running throughout between Edinburgh and London. It was interesting to find that in this brief period some of the 'non-corridor' engines were used. On these occasions the train made one passenger stop, at Newcastle, and there the engine was remanned. On the day when I was a passenger the engine was the celebrated Kings Cross participant in the 1925 Interchange Trials with the GWR, No 4474 *Victor Wild*. She had a far harder

'The Flying Scotsman'
Load: 14 coaches, 445 tons tare 475 tons full
Engine: 4—6—2 No 4474 *Victor Wild*

Dist miles			Sch min	Actual m s	Speeds mph
0.0	EDINBURGH (WAVERLEY)	.	0	0 00	—
3.0	Portobello	. .		4 58	—
6.5	Inveresk	.		8 57	62/53
17.8	Drem Jc	.		20 43	69
23.4	East Linton	.		25 56	60/69
29.1	DUNBAR	.	34	31 09	—
33.8	Innerwick	.		35 49	62½
41.2	Grantshouse	.		47 06	27
51.9	Burnmouth	.		57 26	71 (max)
57.5	BERWICK	.	67	63 15	25 *
63.6	Goswick	.		70 30	68½
—				pws	
65.8	Beal	. .		73 10	35 *
78.4	Chathill	.		87 52	66
83.4	*Milepost 41*	.		91 50	51½
89.6	ALNMOUTH	.	101	98 54	72/44 *
101.2	Widdrington	.		111 50	69
107.8	MORPETH	.	121½	118 22	35 *
114.5	Cramlington	.		126 23	60/54
—				pws	42 *
119.4	Forest Hall	.		131 56	64 (max)
124.4	NEWCASTLE	.	144	139 46	

137 min Net   *speed restrictions

'The Flying Scotsman'
Load: 14 coaches, 445 tons tare, 475 tons full
Engine: 4—6—2 No 4474 *Victor Wild*

Dist miles			Sch min	Actual m s	Speeds mph
0.0	NEWCASTLE	.	0	0 00	—
8.2	Chester-le-Street	.		11 58	—
14.0	Durham	.	20½	19 17	—
36.0	DARLINGTON	.	48	46 02	60/56 *
41.2	*Eryholme Jc*	.		51 20	64/57
50.1	NORTHALLERTON		63	60 17	—
57.9	Thirsk	.	70	67 32	69
68.9	Alne	.		77 17	72
77.1	*Milepost 3*	. .		84 23	67½
80.1	YORK	.	90½	88 50	20 *
89.8	Riccall	. .		100 56	64½
93.9	SELBY	.	108	105 35	25 *
102.3	Balne	.		115 20	66
108.1	Shaftholme Jc	.		120 43	64½
112.3	DONCASTER	.	128	125 04	53 *
129.7	RETFORD	.	145	144 02	easy
134.5	*Markham Box*	.		150 05	44
140.9	Crow Park	.		155 58	76½
148.2	NEWARK	.	163½	162 02	68½
162.8	GRANTHAM	.	179	177 44	46/51
168.2	*Stoke Box*	.		185 18	38
179.7	Essendine	.		195 09	84
188.8	*Werrington Jc*	.		202 27	71
191.9	PETERBOROUGH		207	205 54	20 *
198.9	Holme	.		214 15	69
204.8	Abbots Ripton	.		219 49	53
209.4	HUNTINGDON	.	226½	224 21	76½
216.6	St Neots	.		230 23	62½
227.2	Biggleswade	.		240 03	70 (max)
236.4	HITCHIN	.	251	249 38	48½
239.7	Stevenage	.		254 12	41
243.3	Knebworth	.		258 33	53/51
250.6	HATFIELD	.	266	265 29	74
255.6	Potters Bar	.		270 18	60
259.1	New Barnet	.		273 28	74
263.3	Wood Green	.		276 49	76½
265.7	Finsbury Park	.		279 00	
268.3	KINGS CROSS	.	286	283 20	

*Speed restrictions

The down 'non-stop' on Langley troughs near Stevenage: engine No 4475 *Flying Fox*

THE GRESLEY PACIFICS

Engine No 4472 'off duty': working the 4.15 pm down semi-fast from Kings Cross on Langley troughs.
This was a regular turn for the London No 1 link engines and men

task than when the 'non-stop' was first introduced. There was first of all a 14-coach train of 475 tons gross trailing load, and in 1936, when this run was made the schedule was a full hour faster, inclusive of the 5 min stop at Newcastle:

Edinburgh–Newcastle, 124.4 miles, 144 min 51.8 mph

Newcastle–Kings Cross, 268.3 miles, 286 min 56.3 mph

Throughout the run there never seemed any sign that the engine was requiring to be nursed, or the coal or water supply giving anxiety.

I do not know who the driver was on the first stage, but as the accompanying log shows he started in dashing style and was through Dunbar nearly 3 min early. The Cockburnspath bank was climbed well, with a lowest speed of 27 mph on the long 1 in 96 gradient, and with some brisk running to follow Berwick was passed $3\frac{3}{4}$ min early. A permanent way check at Beal came at the foot of the long gradual rise to the top of the Christon bank, at milepost 41, but despite this hindrance the train was still comfortably ahead of time at Alnmouth, where the speed reduction was much more pronounced than usual. Further good running brought the 'Flying Scotsman' into Newcastle $4\frac{1}{4}$ min early with a net time of 137 min from Edinburgh— an average speed of 54.5 mph. This early arrival, plus the 5 min scheduled stop certainly gave time for a thorough examination of the engine, and on the earlier stages of the long non-stop run to London, Driver Sheen of Kings Cross

certainly took advantage of the relatively ample schedule to work the engine under easy steam. With complete absence of checks we were gradually gaining time, and having passed Doncaster nearly 3 min early he ran very easily on to Retford.

The final stage, from Grantham to Kings Cross, was by far the sharpest timed, with only 107 min for the last 105.5 miles, and it was as though the driver was running as close as possible to his booked point-to-point times throughout rather than getting time in hand on the easy stretches so as to be able to relax, so to speak, on the last stages. Thus we passed Grantham, only $1\frac{1}{4}$ min ahead, though as the log shows there was close observance of all the subsequent intermediate times. Note should be taken of the maximum speed of 84 mph down the Essendine bank; of the vigorous recovery from the Peterborough slack, and the excellent finish whereby we stopped in Kings Cross $2\frac{3}{4}$ min early. By contrast to the leisurely running required when the 'non-stop' was first put on, this timing required an average speed of 58.5 mph from passing Darlington to arriving in Kings Cross. The net running times on this fine journey totalled no more than 420 min, an average of 56.1 mph. This was in some ways a farewell trip for the non-streamlined 'Pacifics' on the London–Edinburgh through workings because in the following season the 'non-stop' was taken over by the new streamlined 'A4' engines.

CHAPTER 7

THE 'A3' CLASS

The developments in valve gear design, and the first experiments with higher boiler pressures described in Chapter 5 had their outcome in a batch of ten new 'Pacifics', the first of which was completed at Doncaster in August 1928. While the second high pressure engine No 2544 *Lemberg* with $18\frac{1}{4}$ in diameter cylinders had proved extremely fast, and a remarkably light coal-burner it was felt that advantage could be taken of the steam raising capacity of the boiler, with its higher superheat, to increase the nominal tractive effort, and the cylinders of the new engines were made 19 in. This raised the tractive effort to 32,909 lb at 85 per cent boiler pressure. This new series was, in effect, the consummation of the non-streamlined 'Pacific' design, and although the basic changes from the original 180 lb engines, classed 'A1', are well-known, there were a number of very important changes in detail design, some of which arose from the experience in running non-stop between Kings Cross and Newcastle.

Foremost among these changes were those made to the lubrication, and the design of such vital bearings as the big ends. The original Great Northern 'Pacifics' had solid big ends on the outside connecting rods, with a brass bush with whitemetal liners dovetailed in, as shown in the drawing on page 34. The design of the 'A3' connecting rod is shown on page 92, and has a floating bush of solid bronze, without any white-metal insertions, and lubrication to the inner surface was through 24 holes $\frac{1}{4}$ in diameter spaced as shown in the subsidiary view of the 'development' of the outside face of the bronze bush. The inside big end, which was of the marine type, as on the 'A1' engines, necessarily had split bearings, and these were provided with pockets into which the whitemetal linings were cast. The connecting rods of the 'A3' engines, shown in the drawing on page 92, had whitemetal linings on all the bearings.

Another interesting change in design from that of the 'A1' class was in respect of the pistons

The first of the standard 'A3' class: No 2743 *Felstead*

THE GRESLEY PACIFICS

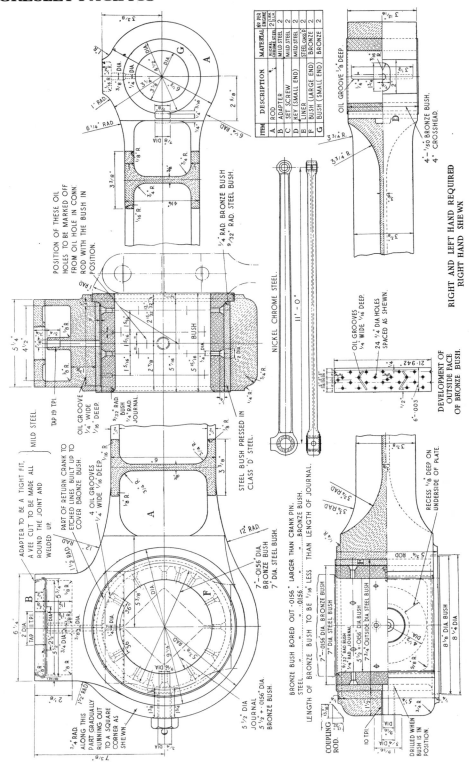

Connecting rod of the 'A3' engines, showing improvements in bearing and lubrication

92

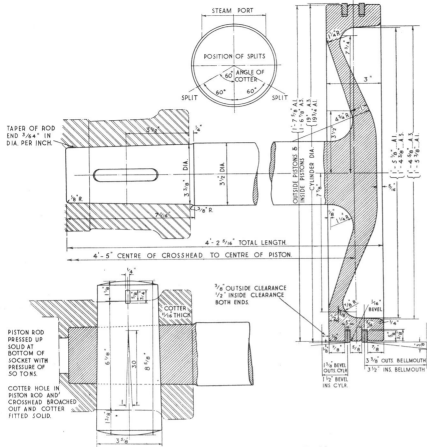

Piston of the 'A3' Pacifics

and their rods. On the 'A1' engines, as shown on page 36, the piston rods were made hollow, and quite a feature was made of this, in the specification originally published, as a means of saving weight. The modified design used on the 'A3' class is shown above. The rod was made solid, but a more important change is to be seen in the form of the piston rings. On the 'A1' class the pistons had a gun metal ring cast on to the piston head, to accommodate two cast iron rings each $\frac{3}{4}$ in wide. In the new engines the piston heads were solid, and contained two narrow rings only. It was a much simpler design, and proved very effective in service. As opportunity came pistons of similar design were fitted to all the 'Pacifics' having 20 in diameter cylinders.

The principal change from the 'A1' class was of course in respect of the boiler. The external shape was not changed in any way, but to provide for the higher pressure the plates were $\frac{23}{32}$ in thick instead of $\frac{5}{8}$ in, the rivets in the longitudinal lap joints between the front and rear rings, and between the rearward ring and the firebox casing remained at $\frac{15}{16}$ in in both boilers. The fireboxes were identical in both classes of locomotive. There was a slight re-arrangement of the tubes from that used in the first 220 lb boilers. The new standard 'A3s' had 125 instead of 121 small tubes, which increased the total evaporative heating surface from 2692 to 2736.6 sq ft; the superheater, still with 43 elements, had a slightly increased heating surface, from 703 to 706 sq ft. The combined total was thus 3442.6 sq ft. The sectional drawings reproduced on pages 94 to 95 show a number of points of minor detail, but the main difference from the operating point of view was in changing the driver's position from the right to the left hand side of the footplate.

This had been a point of some mild controversy between the different railways of Britain, and on formation of the 'groups' in 1923, all—excepting of course the Great Western—had

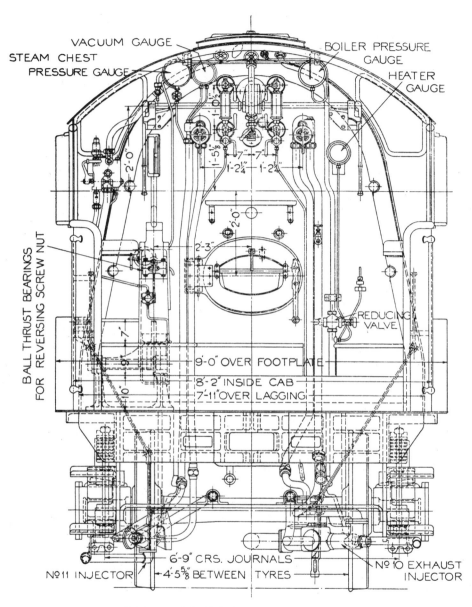

Cab layout of the 'A3' class, arranged for left hand drive

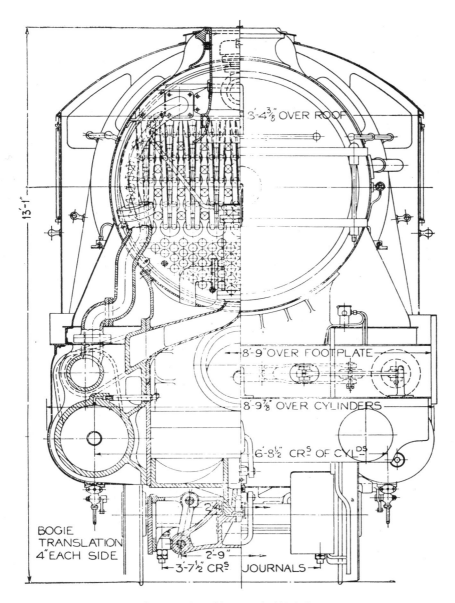

Cross-section of front-end of 'A3' class

THE GRESLEY PACIFICS

major constituents firmly wedded to driving from different sides of the cab. On the LNER all the principal English constituents—Great Eastern, Great Northern, Great Central and North Eastern—drove from the right hand side; it was only in Scotland that left hand drive was favoured. But although the widespread introduction of colour light signalling was a long way ahead in 1928, the majority of far-seeing railwaymen already saw that it was a definite development of the future, and with colour light signalling, left hand drive on a steam locomotive, especially with one having the size of boiler fitted to the Gresley 'Pacifics', was highly desirable. It was nevertheless many years before the earlier 'Pacifics' were changed, and it was indeed the combination of a right-hand drive engine, with colour-light signalling that led indirectly, to the nearest miss from a terrible collision at Northallerton, in 1935.

The first of the new engines was No 2743 *Felstead*, completed at Doncaster in August 1928. After the first two these engines came out roughly at monthly intervals, the last of the ten being out-shopped in April 1929. Their names and numbers were:

2743	*Felstead*	2748	*Colorado*
2744	*Grand Parade*	2749	*Flamingo*
2745	*Captain Cuttle*	2750	*Papyrus*
2746	*Fairway*	2751	*Humorist*
2747	*Coronach*	2752	*Spion Kop*

Like the majority of their predecessors they were named after racehorses, mostly Derby winners, and their distribution on the line was at first:

Doncaster; 2743, 2747, 2751, 2752
Kings Cross; 2744, 2746, 2750
Carlisle (Canal); 2745, 2748, 2749

Since the introduction of 3rd class sleeping cars on the Anglo-Scottish night trains the loads of the principal expresses had grown beyond the unpiloted limit for the North British 'Atlantics', and the drafting of three 'Pacifics' to Carlisle reduced the double-heading that had become frequent, in the height of the season. At Kings Cross *Grand Parade* and the immortal *Papyrus* were to win fame as great runners, while of the Doncaster quartet *Humorist* later became the guinea-pig for experiments with a strange diversity of smoke-deflecting devices, but after the period of this book.

The new engines were not long in showing what they could do, although in almost every area they worked turn and turn about with the 'A1s'. The exception, of course, was on the Waverley route, in Scotland, where the three Carlisle engines had the road to themselves. The 'A1s', with long travel gear, were doing excellent work, and it seemed that everywhere the two varieties of 'Pacific' were allocated indiscriminately. At the same time the period from 1928 to 1931 witnessed some extraordinary

Unusual duty for a Doncaster-based engine: No 2743 *Felstead* on the up 'Flying Scotsman'

A Carlisle 'A3' No 2748 *Colorado* with headboard 'St Pancras' photographed at Haymarket shed

variation in the quality of running made on different parts of the line. I have used the word 'running' rather than performance because I believe the thermodynamic working of the locomotives was uniformly excellent. But there seems to have been a vast disparity in the keenness with which individual engine crews set about their tasks. It was not anything in the

A Doncaster 'A3' No. 2752 *Spion Kop*

THE GRESLEY PACIFICS

shape of 'ca-canny' when the working of heavy loads was concerned; some of the finest runs were made in the most extreme conditions of loading. It suggested, moreover, a collective 'pact' at some shed to avoid anything that looked remotely like making up lost time, no matter how favourable the circumstances might have been.

Most of this apparent lack of spirit was centred on Tyneside. It was so consistent and long sustained as to lead experienced commentators to question whether or not there were particular difficulties being experienced in the working of heavy trains north of York. Cecil J. Allen suggested that 'a false estimate of the character of locomotive performance on any particular trip may be made because the recorder is not acquainted with special circumstances influencing the driver's methods'. He went on to mention the relatively long distances between water troughs on the northern part of the East Coast Route, namely the $96\frac{1}{2}$ miles from Wiske Moor to Lucker, and the 76 miles from the latter on to Edinburgh. In order to take advantage of the high working efficiency of the locomotives certain very long daily turns were scheduled, as between Newcastle and Grantham, and back, and between Edinburgh and York—in certain cases with re-manning en route. Allen refers particularly to the distance between Lucker and Wiske Moor, which he said: '. . . affects not only the "Scotsman" when running non-stop, but this and other winter workings in which the same engine works through Newcastle without change, in the event

of taking water not being conveniently possible there.'

Fair enough, but this would not have explained the situation prevailing for many, many months on a train like the 5.30 pm Newcastle express from Kings Cross, on which the NE Area engines came on fresh at York, and went no farther than Newcastle anyway. Of this train Allen wrote in 1930: 'On the bulk of the journeys it was at Grantham that the enterprising feats of driving began. From Kings Cross to Grantham, which is easily the hardest part of the schedule throughout to Newcastle, drivers were content, for the most part, to keep their net times, regaining no loss by signal checks; from York northwards, on the easiest of the bookings, running was so slack that it was difficult to believe that the same type of locomotive was at the head of the train.' At this time there were certain 'cyclic' diagrams operated alternately by engines from Grantham and Gateshead sheds and some of the engines coming on ostensibly 'fresh' at York, and quoted by Allen as doing so poorly were actually Grantham units, in 'foreign' hands. I know from later experience elsewhere there was nothing like cyclic diagrams with multiple manning to knock the heart out of engine crews. Locomotives did not receive the care and attention they needed, particularly if, as I have often heard said: 'It's not one of ours!' This, added to the traditional 'sales resistance' of NE men to Great Northern locomotives may have explained a good deal of the attitude that was so deplorably apparent. In the period 1928–30

On the Waverley Route: St Pancras–Edinburgh express descending from Whitrope to Hawick hauled by 4—6—2 No 2745 *Captain Cuttle*

5.45 pm Leeds express near Hadley Wood, hauled by No 2747 *Coronach*

the fires of discontent may have been further stoked by the fact that Gateshead did not get any of the first batch of the new 'A3s'.

Turning now to the actual performances of the new engines, pride of place must certainly be given to Doncaster shed, which then had the honour of working the fastest start-to-stop schedules then in force over the East Coast Route. This was the 7.50 am breakfast car express from Leeds to Kings Cross, which in the winter of 1928–9 was booked to run the 105.5 miles from Grantham to Kings Cross in 111 min—an average speed of 57.0 mph. Engines of both 'A1' and 'A3' classes were used indiscriminately as everywhere else, and splendid runs are on record with the two original GNR 'Pacifics' in this same period. But I must give prominence to the tremendous running of one of the new engines, No 2747 *Coronach*. By East Coast standards this was not one of the heaviest of trains, and its normal formation was one of only ten coaches, with a gross trailing load of about 340 tons. With this load *Great Northern*, the pioneer of them all, had dashed up to London in 103¾ min, and her finishing time of 2 min 58 sec, for the final 2.6 miles from Finsbury Park into 'The Cross'—as all GNR men called it—reminds me of the acid comment of Tom Blades, when he was learning the road prior to the 1923 Interchange Trials between GNR and NER 'Pacifics': 'One of those Great Northern b......s will land in Piccadilly Circus one day!'

LNER 9.44 AM GRANTHAM–KINGS CROSS
Load: 51 axles, 356 tons tare, 380 tons full
Engine: Class 'A3' 4—6—2 No 2747 *Coronach*

Dist miles		Sch min	Actual m s	Speeds mph
0.0	GRANTHAM . .	0	0 00	—
5.4	*Stoke Box* . .		9 45	45
8.4	Corby . .		12 45	72½
13.3	Little Bytham .		16 30	88½
16.9	Essendine . .		19 00	86½
20.7	Tallington . .		21 45	83½
26.0	*Werrington Jc* .		25 50	75
29.1	PETERBOROUGH .	31	29 15	20 *
36.1	Holme . .		37 50	67
42.0	Abbots Ripton .		43 30	53½
46.6	HUNTINGDON .	50	48 00	76½
49.5	Offord . .		50 20	75
53.8	St Neots . .		53 55	66
58.0	Tempsford . .		57 35	73½
64.4	Biggleswade . .		63 05	71
69.8	Three Counties .		68 00	66
73.6	HITCHIN . .	77	71 40	57
76.9	Stevenage . .		75 35	49½
80.5	Knebworth . .		79 25	57
87.8	HATFIELD . .	92	86 00	76½
92.8	Potters Bar . .		90 50	59
96.3	New Barnet . .		94 05	75
100.5	Wood Green . .		97 20	79
102.9	Finsbury Park .		99 30	
			sigs.	
105.5	KINGS CROSS . .	111	104 10	

*Speed restriction
Net time: 103 min

However, to revert once again to the 'A3s', the work of *Coronach* is tabulated. To cope with an unexpected rush of passengers extra coaches were added at Grantham, and apparently all that could be found at short notice, were a non-corridor Gresley 'twin', and what the recorder described as 'a pre-historic six-wheeler' —the type that the inimitable E. L. Ahrons once averred had octagonal wheels! This latter vintage specimen was the very last vehicle in the train. The marshalling of these 'extras' made the train 6 min late in leaving Grantham; but despite this, and the load being heavier than normal the train would have been 2 min early at Kings Cross if it had not experienced a signal check right at the finish. Starting well from Grantham, and climbing briskly to Stoke *Coronach* developed some tremendous speed downhill towards Peterborough, with a maximum of $88\frac{1}{2}$ mph below Little Bytham and an average of 81.3 mph over the 15.2 miles from Corby to Helpston Box. Then after the Peterborough slack the effort was kept up without a break, with an average of 67.1 mph over the undulating, but, if anything, slightly adverse 33.7 miles from Holme to Three Counties, and good climbing to Stevenage and to Potters Bar. The net time of 103 min is based on a probable unchecked concluding $3\frac{1}{2}$ min from Finsbury Park into Kings Cross. This would be considered almost dangerously fast today, but was common enough when the 'A3s' were new.

It is striking evidence of the change that was to come over our sense of values in locomotive performance in the 1930s that an early run of one of the London 'A3s', No 2744 *Grand Parade*, should, in 1929, have been described by Cecil J. Allen as 'no mean feat'. She was working the up 'Flying Scotsman', with a 420-ton load, on the winter schedule, and from the start at Darlington ran to a signal stop at Beningbrough, 38.6 miles in 38 min 10 sec start to stop. Over the 24 miles between Northallerton and Milepost 6 the average speed was 71.6 mph with a maximum of 75 mph at Alne. The engine was in the hands of a London crew, and the performance was considered most exhilarating. Little did we then guess what was in store from 1932 onwards with these same engines—and equally, in every respect, with the 'A1' class! Over this same stretch of line Allen later publicised 'a really good run' with the same train behind another London 'A3', the celebrated 2750 *Papyrus* when, with a 410-ton train, the 44.1 miles from Darlington to York were run in exactly 45

min: a gain of 3 min on schedule. The maximum speed on this run did not exceed $71\frac{1}{2}$ mph.

So far as the Anglo-Scottish and the London–Newcastle trains were concerned, it was the 'A1s' that were really stealing the show at that time, through the enterprise of the Grantham top-link drivers; but *Grand Parade* came once again into the picture on that most unlikely of trains, the very heavy, but easily-timed express reaching Kings Cross at 4.30 pm. On this occasion the 'A3' took over a train of 567 tons tare from a Grantham 'A1' at Peterborough, and left $7\frac{1}{2}$ min late. As the accompanying log shows all but 30 sec of this lateness was made up in a remarkable piece of running, with a train that weighed at least 600 tons behind the tender.

LNER 2.58 PM PETERBOROUGH–KINGS CROSS

Load: 567 tons tare, 600 tons full
Engine: Class 'A3' 4—6—2 No 2744 *Grand Parade*

Dist miles		Sch min	Actual m s	Speeds mph
0.0	PETERBOROUGH .	0	0 00	—
7.0	Holme . .		10 45	59
12.9	Abbots Ripton .		17 30	42
17.5	HUNTINGDON .	24	22 45	66
20.4	Offord . .		25 30	67
24.7	St Neots .		29 30	58
28.9	Tempsford .		33 35	$64\frac{1}{2}$
35.3	Biggleswade . .		39 45	$58\frac{1}{2}$
39.4	Arlesey . .		44 15	57
44.5	HITCHIN .	54	49 45	45
47.8	Stevenage .		54 30	$40\frac{1}{2}$
51.4	Knebworth .		58 50	$52\frac{1}{2}$
58.7	HATFIELD .	72	66 00	74
63.7	Potters Bar .		70 50	58
67.2	New Barnet .		74 15	70
71.4	Wood Green .		77 40	$77\frac{1}{2}$
73.8	Finsbury Park .		79 45	
76.4	KINGS CROSS .	92	85 00	

The driver presumably did not venture to approach Kings Cross like the Doncaster men on the Leeds breakfast car train, and took $5\frac{1}{4}$ min in from Finsbury Park. What *Grand Parade* could do with a lighter train was shown on a run I logged myself, in August 1930, on the 8 pm up from Peterborough—the 5.30 pm from Leeds. The load was 440 tons gross, and she passed Finsbury Park in 74 min 10 sec. There was a bad signal check just afterwards, but despite this we stopped in Kings Cross in 79 min 35 sec—$5\frac{1}{2}$ min early.

Performance that created much interest at the time was that of the 'A3s' allocated to the Waverley Route, and rostered to take 400-ton loads without assistance. This had the effect of reducing, to a considerable extent the double heading that had become necessary, because the maximum load for a North British 'Atlantic' was 290 tons. At the same time loading regulations, both on this line and on the East Coast between Edinburgh and Aberdeen were very strict. This was necessarily so on such lengthy and severe gradients, that were subject to extremes of weather, at times. Double heading with the 'Pacifics' was not allowed on these two routes, though it became common enough between Edinburgh and Newcastle at one time. So, on the Waverley Route, 'Atlantics', double-headed, still had to be used when the tare load exceeded 400 tons. With the 'A3' 'Pacifics' however, the interest in their early work over this route lay in its complete negation of all the attributes of the class which had shown so pronouncedly in running over the East Coast main line. The essence of the task was to maintain speeds of 25 to 30 mph on the long 1 in 70 and 1 in 75 ascents, and not to exceed 60 mph anywhere. Quite unofficially I believe, some slight alterations were made to the valve setting of the three engines stationed at Carlisle, though of course the maximum cut-off in full gear remained at 65 per cent. Regular turns were the down night sleeper from St Pancras, leaving Carlisle at 4.25 am, returning with the up 'Thames–Forth Express', and also with the down 'Thames–Forth Express', and back with the up night 'sleeper'. A variation in the traditional headboards carried was at one time made on these workings. North British practice had always been to indicate the extent only of the *engine* working, and the locomotives of the London

LNER EDINBURGH—CARLISLE

Engine: Class 'A3' 4—6—2 No 2745 *Captain Cuttle*

Train				10.5 am		9.55 pm	
Load, to St Boswells				330/350		353/385	
to Carlisle				363/395		353/385	

Dist miles				Sch min	Actual m s		Actual m s	
0.0	WAVERLEY	.	.	0	0	00	0	00
3.0	Portobello .		.	6	5	03	5	00
8.2	Hardengreen Jc	.	.	13	12	10	12	00
12.0	Gorebridge	.	.		18	10	17	40
16.0	Tynehead .		.		27	23	26	15
17.9	*Falahill Box*	.	.	33	31	54	31	00
—					sigs.		—	
35.5	GALASHIELS	.	.	51	51	22	51	00
3.7	MELROSE	.	.	6	6	00	6	00
3.4	ST BOSWELLS	.	.	7	6	42	5	50
12.2	HAWICK	.	.	17	17	23	19	25 *
3.9	Stobs	.	.		10	27	10	40
7.0	Shankend .		.		16	35	17	20
10.9	*Whitrope Box*	.	.	25	23	47	26	00
13.1	Riccarton Jc	.	.	28	26	51	29	05
21.2	NEWCASTLETON	.	.	37	36	06	38	15
35.8	Longtown Jc	.	.	53	50	55	53	40
—					pws		pws	
45.4	CARLISLE	.	.	66	64	27	68	00

*Schedule 20 min

expresses over the Waverley Route were accordingly labelled 'Carlisle'. With the 'Pacifics', the headboard 'St Pancras' was sometimes carried.

Details of two runs with engine No 2745 *Captain Cuttle* are tabulated herewith. The first on the 10.5 am 'Thames–Forth' express carried a load of 350 tons to St Boswells and 395 tons thereafter while the second, on the night train had a load of 385 tons. The latter included

Pride of Carlisle 'Canal': No 2745 *Captain Cuttle*

an extraordinarily mixed rake, of 9 'eights', and a 12-wheeled 'sleeper' for the Midland line, 2 six-wheelers, and no less than 5 four-wheeled fish vans. The North British people always seemed to find some fish vans to attach to any express train made up otherwise to less than the maximum engine load! On the night train Mr R. A. H. Weight was on the footplate, and details of the engine working provide an interesting sidelight on the way the 'Pacifics' had to be driven over this difficult road. At Hardengreen Junction, where the main ascent to Falahill begins the speeds were around 50 mph and the engine was worked in 35 per cent cut-off, with full regulator until Tynehead, where there was an easing to 30 per cent because the train was getting ahead of time. On the long 1 in 70 ascent, with certain brief easings, speed had varied between 27 and 33 mph but fell to 25 at Falahill summit, due to the easing of the engine. On the day train the working was not quite so vigorous. Speed fell to 24 mph at Gorebridge, and 27 mph at Falahill summit. Very cautious running was made on both trips down to Galashiels.

The ascent from Hawick to Whitrope is another severe test of strength, including much hard climbing at 1 in 80 and 1 in 75, complicated by severe reverse curvature. Both these journeys were made in good weather, and the tale might well have been different in the winter storms. As with the 'Atlantics' the trains were banked out of the platform at Hawick, and on the first run *Captain Cuttle* varied between 25½ and 36 mph on the climb, gaining just over a minute on schedule to Whitrope. On the second journey full regulator and cut-offs between 32 and 35 per cent were not enough to keep time, and a minute was lost. This nevertheless represented tough working for these engines—so totally unlike their accustomed style; knowing, also, how prone they were to slipping on a wet rail one cannot really enthuse over their introduction on this route. The fact that they had to be forcibly restrained over the favourable stretches is another point against their use. One can note the average speeds, on these two runs between Newcastleton and Longtown, namely 60 and 57.6 mph, and reflect upon the speeds normally run between Hitchin and Huntingdon!

Having said that much I must bring the picture of Southern Area performance by those first 'A3s' up to the end of 1930 by tabulating two contrasting runs by the Doncaster-based engines on the favourite racing ground between Kings Cross and Peterborough. The first was on the 1.10 am out of Kings Cross, heavily loaded mostly with newspaper vans, and included so leisurely a start out to Hatfield as to suggest that the engine was in some trouble. Speed fell as low as 32 mph on the climb to Potters Bar, and the train was 5½ min late as early as Hatfield. Then however there came a terrific, long-sustained spurt, with an average

					LNER KINGS CROSS—PETERBOROUGH: 'A3' ENGINES						
Train							1.10 am			1.30 pm	
Engine No							2743			2751	
„ name							*Felstead*			*Humorist*	
Load tons E/F							445/470			509/545	
Dist miles					Sch min	Actual m s		Speeds mph	Actual m s		Speeds* mph
0.0	KINGS CROSS	.	.	.	0	0	00	—	0	00	—
2.6	Finsbury Park	.	.	.		8	15	—	6	22	—
5.0	Wood Green	.	.	.		12	25	—	9	31	—
9.2	New Barnet	.	.	.		19	20	—	14	45	48.1
12.7	Potters Bar	.	.	.		25	15	32	19	35	43.4
17.7	HATFIELD	.	.	.	25	30	30	75	24	45	58.2
23.5	*Woolmer Green*	.	.	.		35	50	52	30	10	64.3
28.6	Stevenage	.	.	.		40	40	—·	34	54	64.6
31.9	HITCHIN	.	.	.	39	43	25	—	37	56	65.3
37.0	Arlesey	.	.	.		47	10	86½	41	55	76.7
44.1	Sandy	.	.	.		52	35	—	48	10	68.2
51.7	St Neots	.	.	.		58	40	72½	55	10	65.1
58.9	HUNTINGDON	.	.	.	64	64	20	78½	61	42	66.2
62.0	*Milepost 62*	.	.	.		67	10	61½	64	56	57.4
69.4	Holme	.	.	.		73	20	80½	71	45	65.2
75.0	*Fletton Jc*	.	.	.		78	00	—	76	55	65.1
76.4	PETERBOROUGH	.	.	.	83	79	45		79	08	

*Average speeds

A striking broadside view of the Gateshead 'A3' No 2595 *Trigo*, at Kings Cross

speed of 74.7 mph over the 44 miles from Stevenage to Yaxley, including a maximum of 86½ mph, and Peterborough was reached just inside 80 min. The second run was on the 1.30 pm with *Humorist*, before any experiments in smoke deflecting had been made to her smokebox. It was a grand effort. The recorder did not take any maximum or minimum speeds, but I have worked out the averages, and include them in the accompanying table. The splendid start, with this 545-ton train put engine and crew completely on top of the job from Hatfield, and time was steadily gained thereafter.

By the New Year of 1930 the next batch of 'A3s' was in production at Doncaster, and these eight engines were completed and allocated as follows:

Engine No	Name	Completed 1930	Shed
2595	*Trigo*	February	Gateshead
2596	*Manna*	February	,,
2597	*Gainsborough*	April	,,
2598	*Blenheim*	April	,,
2795	*Call Boy*	April	Haymarket
2796	*Spearmint*	May	,,
2797	*Cicero*	June	,,
2599	*Book Law*	July	Gateshead

The names were the usual queer mixture, but quite typical of those associated with the Turf. Engine No 2596 took the name displaced when the 'A1' No 2553 was named *Prince of Wales*, but it was the title of No 2796 that really outraged those who had a more sensitive regard for engine names. Famous racehorse it might

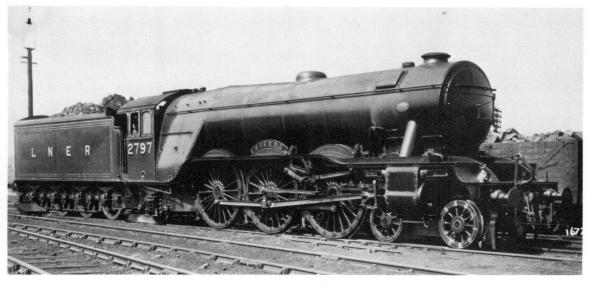

A Haymarket 'A3' No 2797 *Cicero* with the high-sided non-corridor tender

THE GRESLEY PACIFICS

Four 'Pacifics' at Haymarket. Left to right: 2596 *Manna* (A3 Gateshead); 2573 *Harvester* (A3 Gateshead); 2563 *William Whitelaw* (A1 Haymarket); and 2402 *City of York* (Raven type A2)

have been; but to name one of the finest express locomotives in the country after a brand of chewing gum was going too far! By way of a *riposte* one critic suggested that the Great Western might reply by renaming one of the '60XX' class 4—6—0s *King Kong*; it would, he suggested, become a hot favourite for the Cornish Riviera Stakes! Despite this *Spearmint* survived her deprecators; and largely through the literary aspirations of one of her latterday drivers became quite an honoured unit in the stud of the Gresley 'Pacifics'. Of the three that went new to Haymarket in 1930 it was No 2795 *Call Boy* that stole practically all the limelight in those early days. In the way that steam locomotives of the same batch differ individually from each other *Call Boy* was much the best of the three, and she was a consistent favourite on the 'non-stop' Scotsman for several seasons in succession.

The allocation of the three new 'Pacifics' to Haymarket shed, to reinforce the five original engines enabled 'Pacifics' to be rostered to certain turns on the Aberdeen road, and this revived for a time the practice adopted when the Reid 'Atlantics' were new in 1906, of working through unchanged between Waverley and Aberdeen. As on the Carlisle road however, the workings had to be arranged within the maximum tonnages permitted, for the double-heading of 'Pacifics' was forbidden by the civil engineer. The load limits laid down were 480 tons going north, and 440 tons on the south-

bound journey. Although the total vertical rise was naturally the same in both directions, the southbound run had the more awkward gradients, particularly in the starts out of Montrose and Dundee, and the climb from Inverkeithing on to the Forth Bridge. Sometimes return journeys had to be arranged on lightly loaded trains, because the return workings promised tonnages well beyond even the 'Pacific' limits. I went north one day on the morning express from Edinburgh and the 'A1' Pacific No 2566 *Ladas* worked through, being remanned at Dundee. From Kirkcaldy the load, after attaching the Glasgow portion, was 491 tons tare, but a point was evidently stretched and the 'Pacific' took this on to Dundee unaided. Onwards to Aberdeen, with a different engine crew, the load was reduced to 353 tons tare, within the 'Atlantic' load. The 'Pacific' would ordinarily have worked back on the 3.45 pm train from Aberdeen; but that train was over the maximum of 440 tons allowed, and the 'Pacific' had to be held back for the much lighter 5.45 pm.

There did not seem to be much point in these through engine workings, and they were soon abandoned. An equivalent daily mileage could be obtained from the Haymarket engines by making two return trips to Dundee, which had previously been worked with 'Atlantics', and was subsequently adopted with 'Pacifics' and the 'P2' 2—8—2s. The use of 'Pacifics' on the Aberdeen road, both north and south of Dundee, with little chance of settling down to spells of sustained fast running, was not an ideal arrangement, and the restriction of loads was a clear indication of the severity of the conditions imposed. In a later chapter, some footplate observations of my own on 'A3' Pacifics between Edinburgh and Dundee make a very strong contrast to what was customary then south of Newcastle. The Haymarket engines filled in their mileage with certain turns to Glasgow, but the schedules were not such as to demand any appreciable effort from locomotives of such power and competence. On the 9.45 pm from Queen Street, conveying the through sleeping car portion from Fort William to Kings Cross, No. 2797 *Cicero*, after climbing to Cowlairs, 1.6 miles in 5 min 40 sec, took 28¼ min to cover the ensuing level miles to the stop at Polmont, 23.4 miles farther on, with no higher speed than 58½ mph, and a train of 350 tons. The continuation was rather better, as from the restart we passed Haymarket West Junction, 20 miles, in 21 min 25 sec and stopped in Waverley 22.3 miles in 26 min 5 sec. Even so, the speed at no time exceeded 66 mph.

The new engines allocated to Gateshead did not at first work regularly into London; but before the notable speed-up of 1932, which is dealt with in the next chapter, a different arrangement of long-mileage working was adopted, with highly beneficial results. Instead of 'cyclic' diagrams, with engines worked by two or more crews in the course of a single round of duty, the Tyneside sheds were put into direct competition with Kings Cross on a

2795 *Call Boy* passing Northallerton with the up 'non-stop'

series of double-home turns which were made with the same engines. The trains concerned were, northbound, the 10 am, 1.20 pm and 5.30 pm departures from Kings Cross, and the 8 am up from Newcastle together with the up 'Flying Scotsman', and the up afternoon Scotsman. Normally Kings Cross men worked the three trains down on Mondays, Wednesdays and Fridays, returning each case on the following day. Heaton men worked the 8 am up from Newcastle, and the down 'Flying Scotsman', while Gateshead had the remaining two turns. The inclusion of Heaton shed was interesting, and I was to record some exceptionally fine work from the small, but very keen link of drivers stationed there. So far as Gateshead was

Aberdeen-London express leaving York with engine No 2599 *Book Law*: note, the leading coach is an ex-NBR vehicle

THE GRESLEY PACIFICS

Kings Cross, 10 am: the down non-stop Scotsman leaving behind engine No 2795 *Call Boy*: at far left No 2549 *Persimmon* on 10.10 am Newcastle express, in centre No 2579 *Dick Turpin* on the 10.5 am 'Junior Scotsman'

concerned the change wrought a positive transformation, as the next chapter will show.

I have written so enthusiastically about the Haymarket 'A3' *Call Boy*, that although it is stepping over a little into the period of the next chapter, I conclude this preliminary account of the 'A3s' and their work with details of a run on the 'non-stop' Scotsman, made after the schedule had been cut to $7\frac{1}{2}$ hours. The load was much heavier than when the 'non-stop' was first introduced in 1928. On this run we had fourteen coaches on, and with practically every seat reserved in advance the gross trailing load was at least 480 tons. The details are tabulated in two halves, corresponding to the spells of duty of the two engine crews; the actual changeover took place as usual at Tollerton. The schedule involved running hard to Grantham, to keep out of the way of the 10.5 am Junior Scotsman, and then 'killing time' on to York, to avoid approaching that station the least amount ahead of time. As it was we experienced adverse signals, but by good judgment our driver hung back sufficiently for the road to be cleared just in time, and a dead stand avoided. It will be noticed however that the running as far as Peterborough was fully up to

the best standards of the Leeds trains, on which the Doncaster 'Pacifics' had only 156 miles to go, instead of 393.

The changeover of enginemen was made at exactly 60 mph and after the enforced dawdling from Grantham the pace became distinctly brisker for a while, touching 66 mph at Thirsk, 68 at Danby Wiske and $70\frac{1}{2}$ mph at Croft Spa. By Durham, indeed, we were $4\frac{1}{4}$ min early, and most of this had to be let slip to avoid approaching Newcastle out of our correct path. Once through that critical area without a stop we made some fine running on to Berwick. It was after Alnmouth that I was able to go through the corridor tender and spend just over half an hour on the footplate. The engine had then been at work for nearly 6 hr, and I found everything spick and span, plenty of coal left on the tender, and the engine purring along at 15 per cent cut-off, with the regulator something less than full open. At Lucker troughs we got a full tender, and we went skimming down to the seashore at Beal at 75 mph. Berwick was passed nearly 6 min early, and the driver justifiably did not press the engine on the lengthy ascent to Grantshouse, where the summit was passed at 39 mph, working at 18 per cent cut-off. It certainly

LNER THE NON-STOP 'FLYING SCOTSMAN'
STAGE ONE: KINGS CROSS—TOLLERTON

Engine: Class 'A3' 4—6—2 No 2795 *Call Boy*

Dist miles		Sch min	Actual m s	Speeds mph
0.0	KINGS CROSS	0	0 00	—
5.0	Wood Green		10 52	53
9.2	New Barnet		16 23	43
12.7	Potters Bar		21 08	46
17.7	HATFIELD	25	26 02	75
23.5	*Woolmer Green*		31 13	59
31.9	HITCHIN	39	38 49	76
41.1	Biggleswade		45 54	82 (max)
51.7	St Neots		54 22	66
58.9	HUNTINGDON	61	60 23	74½/55
69.4	Holme		70 07	72½
76.4	PETERBOROUGH	79	78 15	10 *
88.6	Essendine		94 11	58 (max)
100.1	*Stoke Box*		107 43	46
105.5	GRANTHAM	114	113 22	60
120.1	NEWARK	130	129 03	60
133.7	*Markham Box*		144 19	46
138.6	RETFORD	151	149 27	64½
149.5	*Milepost 149½*		161 25	48/63
156.0	DONCASTER	170	168 48	40 *
169.8	Templehirst		185 30	61¼
174.4	SELBY	191	190 30	33 *
—			sigs	
188.2	YORK	209	209 20	15 *
193.7	Beningbrough		216 55	57
197.9	Tollerton		221 17	60

*Reductions of speed

STAGE TWO: TOLLERTON—EDINBURGH

Dist miles		Sch min	Actual m s	Speeds mph
197.9	Tollerton		221 17	60
210.4	Thirsk	234	233 33	66
218.2	Northallerton	242	240 27	61/68
227.1	*Eryholme Jc*		249 20	62/70½
232.3	DARLINGTON	256	254 01	65
237.7	Aycliffe		259 36	60/52
245.2	Ferryhill		267 36	62
250.1	Croxdale		272 17	70½
254.3	DURHAM	282	277 40	25 *
260.1	Chester-le-Street		285 14	62 (max)
267.7	*King Edward Bridge Jc*		294 38	
268.3	NEWCASTLE	300	298 25	5 *
273.3	Forest Hall		307 32	—
278.2	Cramlington		315 03	44
284.9	MORPETH	325	322 53	30 *
288.5	Longhirst		327 17	63/58
296.8	Acklington		335 19	69
303.1	ALNMOUTH	345	341 03	65
307.7	Little Mill		346 22	42½
314.3	Chathill		353 12	69
319.9	Belford	363	358 53	55
326.9	Beal		365 14	75
331.8	Scremerston		369 43	50
335.2	BERWICK	380	374 13	35 *
340.8	Burnmouth		386 53	—
346.4	Reston Jc		394 15	53
351.5	Grantshouse		401 51	39
358.9	Innerwick		409 25	82½
363.6	DUNBAR		413 20	45 *
374.9	Drem Jc		425 13	64/53
386.2	Inveresk		437 02	63½
389.7	Portobello		441 32	
392.7	EDINBURGH (WAVERLEY)	450	447 23	

The up 'non-stop' Flying Scotsman near Grantham, hauled by No 2795 *Call Boy*

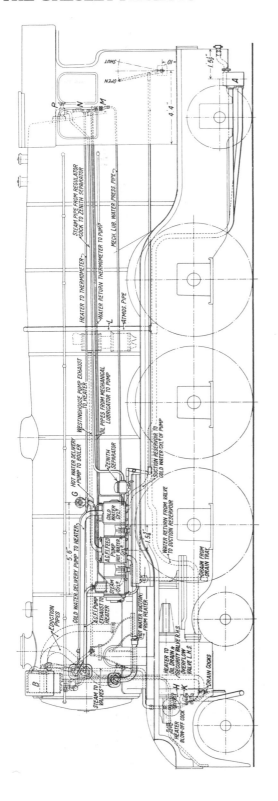

needed no encouragement from the driver for the engine to dash effortlessly down the Cockburnspath bank at $82\frac{1}{2}$ mph and on passing Dunbar, with 29.1 miles of slightly undulating track to go we had $36\frac{1}{2}$ min left in which to make a punctual arrival. We were dawdling once again, and as we came sedately over the last 3 miles from Portobello into Waverley, taking nearly 6 min over them, I thought of the last hectic night in the Race to the North, when Tom Blades was firing to Bob Nicholson, and that same 3 miles took no more than 3 min. *Call Boy* brought the non-stop into Waverley just over $2\frac{1}{2}$ min early after a well-nigh immaculate run.

It is nevertheless interesting to try and analyse how much time might have been gained, had it been necessary, if the various intermediate speed restrictions had been run through at normal speed, instead of funereally slow, as at Doncaster, Selby, York, Newcastle, Morpeth and Berwick—not to mention the final run in from Portobello. Comparing these times with a post-war run, when the engine was short of steam, and the driver was anxious to snatch every second he could, when it did not involve extra steam consumption, I calculate that a total of $12\frac{1}{2}$ min was 'given away' in trying to fill out the time, and that if the road had been clear we could, without burning one extra lump of coal, have run non-stop from Kings Cross to Waverley in 435 min. It was a truly splendid demonstration of the long-distance capacity of the Gresley 'Pacifics'.

The importance of reducing, still further, the coal consumption received constant attention from Gresley and his staff, and the striking economies that had been effected on certain large American locomotives by the application of feed-water heating, notably on the Pennsylvania, had led to trials of the ACFI apparatus and its standardisation on the 'B 12' 4—6—0s of the former Great Eastern Railway. In 1929 what was termed an 'improved' type of ACFI apparatus was fitted to two 'Pacifics', a 220 lb engine, No 2580 *Shotover*, and a 180 lb engine No 2576 *The White Knight*. Both engines were then based in the North Eastern Area, and both had the Westinghouse brake. Compared to the ex-GER 4—6—0s, which had large reservoirs

Diagram of ACFI feed water heating apparatus on 'A3' engine No 2580 *Shotover*

108

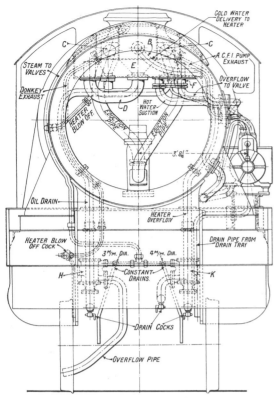

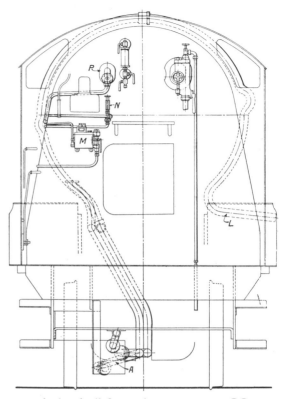

A Suction vessel, fed by gravity from tender
B Mixing chamber, where cold water mingles with exhaust steam from blast pipe
CC The oil separators
D Connection pipe
E Hot water chamber
F Overflow pipe
G Clack valve
H Oil drain and security valve, evacuates drained oil from the separators, CC
K Return valve
L Atmospheric pipe, prevents excess pressure being built up in the system
M Mechanical lubricator
N Thermometer, indicating feed water temperature
P Steam regulator cock, for adjusting the speed of the pump.

Left hand side view of No 2580 showing arrangement of ACFI apparatus

Standard style of the 1930s: engine No 4479 *Robert the Devil*, with long-travel valves, number on cab side, but retaining original-height boiler mountings

carried on the top of the boiler, the improved arrangement on the two 'Pacifics' was a great deal neater. The schematic layout of the equipment can be seen from the drawings reproduced on pages 108–9. The heater was arranged to fit into the smokebox ahead of the chimney, and this not only made for a neat external layout, but it largely eliminated the heat losses by radiation that occurred with the two circular reservoirs mounted on top of the boiler, as on the GER 4—6—0s.

The experiment was not extended beyond the two engines 2576 and 2580. It was evident that this arrangement did not show any marked increase in efficiency over the standard method of boiler feed on the 'Pacifics', with one live and one exhaust steam injector, both of which are, of course, effective feed water heaters in themselves.

The 180 lb Pacific with ACFI apparatus: No 2576 *The White Knight* on 7.25 am Kings Cross–Edinburgh express near East Fortune

CHAPTER 8

LONG AWAITED SPEED-UP : 1932 ONWARDS

If one looks back at the full history of the Gresley 'Pacifics', the first ten years, from the completion of the *Great Northern* to the momentous May of 1932, can appear as a time of 'dress rehearsal'. There were the early tests; the changes in detail design, and the developments in valve gear and boilers. There was the great venture of the Edinburgh 'non-stop', the distribution of the new engines over the entire East Coast route, and periods in which ex-North Eastern, and ex-North British drivers were familiarising themselves with all the working features of the engines, and getting to form *their own* appreciation of their merits. By the end of 1930, with 70 of them in service, and 67 of those exclusively on the East Coast route, the stage was set for their capacity to be utilised to its fullest advantage, to the benefit of the travelling public. Yet, withal, the times were not exactly propitious. The country was in the depths of the most serious trade depression in history. Tyneside, from which so much of LNER traffic normally came, was most grievously affected, and with the depression being world-wide, tourist traffic and particularly that derived from American visitors was at a low ebb.

Yet it was at this time that the management of the LNER, in close harmony with that of the LMS decided to trim drastically the age-old 'gentleman's agreement' on minimum times from London to the Scottish cities, and to embark on a very striking acceleration programme. Here, of course, I am concerned only with the demands it made upon the locomotives. The running of the trains during the ensuing years was very fully documented in contemporary railway literature, but while details of point-to-point times and high speeds delighted an ever-growing army of amateur enthusiasts—to such an extent that one, whose partisan loyalties lay elsewhere suggested, sarcastically, that the Stephenson Locomotive Society should be renamed the Gresley Locomotive Society—the full significance of what was going on can best be appreciated by a more analytical approach. Technically, the period from 1932–7 witnessed the full flowering of the Gresley design-development on the 'A1' and 'A3' engines; yet at the same time the high utilisation and heavy continuous steaming began to reveal certain weaknesses, that were perhaps inevitable in locomotives built in the conditions that prevailed in Doncaster works. Not a great deal had been done to modernise production methods, though I must add at once that the quality of individual workmanship was second to none. Nevertheless the clearances that had to be allowed sometimes took their toll!

In view of the frequency with which very high speeds were attained on favourable stretches of line, with maximum load trains a word must be added about gravitational effects on various gradients. Standard East Coast coaching stock was beautifully designed, and free running, and one can be very sure that Gresley, as a former carriage and wagon engineer, took as much interest in minimising coach resistance as he did in maximising locomotive power. The stock used on the principal expresses probably had specific resistances differing not very much from the post-nationalisation BR figures. In the higher ranges of speed these were as shown in the table overleaf.

Gravitational resistance, of course, is the weight divided by the inclination, so that on a 1 in 200 gradient it is 2240 lb divided by 200 or

THE GRESLEY PACIFICS

COACH ROLLING RESISTANCE	
Speed mph	Resistance lb per ton
70	10.5
75	11.3
80	12.3
85	13.4
90	14.5

11.2 lb per ton. Corresponding figures are 12.6 lb per ton for a gradient of 1 in 178; 8.5 for 1 in 264, and 6.8 lb per ton for 1 in 330. So that on a 1 in 200 gradient descending at 75 mph the assistance from gravity is just about balancing the rolling resistance of the train. So far as the engine is concerned it might be working light, or hauling a 600-ton train! I know that adverse winds, curves in the track, and other extraneous items can add materially to the resistance; but these fundamental facts about train running must be borne in mind, and not too much glamour bestowed upon high downhill speeds.

A laudable feature about the acceleration programme of 1932 was the preferential treatment given to businessmen's trains, rather than 'show' between-times flyers; and it was the 7.50 am up from Leeds that became the fastest train on the LNER. This had its time over the 105.5 miles from Grantham to Kings Cross cut from 111 to the level 100 min, and demanded a start-to-stop average of 63.3 mph. It carried a minimum tare load of just under 300 tons, and the gross trailing load was usually about 315 tons. This was a fairly light load so far as the

Gresley 'Pacifics' were concerned; no difficulty was experienced in working the train to time with loads up to 400 tons. 'A1' and 'A3' engines were used indiscriminately, though from the numerous published records of the running of the train the honours undoubtedly rested with the 'A3s'. I must admit however that my own personal experiences of the train were not of the happiest. Twice, by the courtesy of Mr I. S. W. Groom, who was then Running Superintendent of the Southern Area, I was favoured with footplate passes, and on both occasions we failed to keep time. On the first an 'A1', No 2543 *Melton*, was steaming poorly, and on the second, with another 'A1', No 2559 *The Tetrarch*, the driver underestimated the effect of a strong cross wind, and lost time badly between Peterborough and Hatfield. The indiscriminate allocation of engines to duties, is sometimes perplexing to the visitor. On the second of these two runs of mine on the 'Breakfast Flyer', as it became known, there was a relief train running ahead, lighter than our train by at least 100 tons. Yet for this latter an 'A3' in spanking condition was provided while we had to make do with an 'A1' that had amassed a considerable mileage since last overhaul. Both were Doncaster engines and both were on simple single-home turns to London.

To show the working of the 'Breakfast Flyer' at its best I have tabulated four runs herewith. The first three had the standard minimum train formation, and it is important to note that a rake of ten vehicles was carried on no more

The Up 'Scarborough Flier' south of New Barnet: engine No 4477 *Gay Crusader*

LNER 9.40 am GRANTHAM–KINGS CROSS

Engine No „ Name Load tons E/F			2555 *Centenary* 297/315		2752 *Spion Kop* 300/315		2544 *Lemberg* 301/315		2751 *Humorist* 360/385	
Dist miles		Sch min	Actual m s	Speeds mph	Actual m s	Speeds mph	Actual m s	Speeds mph	Actual m s	Speeds mph
0.0	GRANTHAM	0	0 00	—	0 00	—	0 00	—	0 00	—
5.4	*Stoke Box*		8 09	50	8 15	48	8 02	52	8 14	47
16.9	Essendine		17 30	79	17 02	90	16 30	93¾	17 43	85
26.0	*Werrington Jc*		24 40	—	23 26	—	22 45	—	24 38	—
29.1	PETERBOROUGH	29	27 51	30*	26 30	—	25 53	20*	27 55	—
36.1	Holme		35 28	74	34 00	75	33 38	76½	35 55	70½
42.0	Abbots Ripton		40 13	64	39 02	62½	38 28	—	41 12	57
			—	—	—	—	sigs		—	
46.6	HUNTINGDON	46	44 25	76	43 03	79	42 57	79	45 32	76½
53.8	St Neots		50 16	—	48 37	—	48 31	72½	51 16	69
61.4	Sandy		56 28	—	54 32	80½	54 30	77½	57 25	77½
64.4	Biggleswade		58 56	—	56 54	—	56 50	—	59 50	—
73.6	HITCHIN	68	66 57	61	64 34	66	64 42	64½	68 00	—
76.9	Stevenage		70 16	59	67 53	58	68 08	56	71 28	56
			pws		—		sigs		—	
87.8	HATFIELD	81	81 01	79	77 25	77½	80 08	67	81 07	80½
92.8	Potters Bar		85 40	62½	81 50	66	84 45	65	85 22	68
100.5	Wood Green		92 13	78	88 22	75	91 05	79	91 20	85
			—		pws		—		—	
102.9	Finsbury Park		94 24	—	91 05	—	93 12	—	93 15	—
			sigs		sigs		sigs			
105.5	KINGS CROSS	100	99 11	—	97 30	—	97 20	—	96 45	—
	Net times		96¾		94		93½		96¾	

*Reductions of speed

than 34 axles. This was due to the use of Gresley's articulated stock, which further reduced the train resistance. There were five ordinary 8-wheelers, a triplet-articulated dining car set, and a 'twin' brake first, 300 tons tare all told. On the first run tabulated, *Centenary*, the first engine to have the Spencer layout of long-travel valves, was still a favourite at Doncaster. She made a remarkable run, showing that with minimum load time could be kept without exceeding 80 mph anywhere, though of course the fine uphill speeds were not difficult to make with a load of no more than 315 tons. On the second run *Spion Kop* went like the wind, and reached a full '90' near Essendine, as well as crossing the '80' mark near Tempsford—an unusual thing in those days.

The second experimental high-pressure engine *Lemberg*, with cylinders lined up to 18¼ in diameter, and piston valves proportionately large in relation to the cylinder volume, had already gained the reputation of being a very free running engine, and this was certainly confirmed on run No 3 in the table. The maximum attained in the descent from Stoke to Werrington was 93¾ mph—the highest that had been recorded with a Gresley 'Pacific', up to midsummer 1933. This run was beset by no fewer than three signal checks, and yet the arrival in

Kings Cross was 2¾ min early. The critical section of this run was always the slightly adverse 27 miles from Huntingdon down to Hitchin, where the rising gradient averaged 1 in 660 and the booked speed was 73.6 mph. The three engines hauling 315-ton loads averaged 71.8, 75.2 and 74.4 mph representing sustained outputs of 900 to 1000 equivalent drawbar horsepower. On the fourth run, where a load of 385 tons was conveyed, the average speed over this section was 72.2 mph and the equivalent drawbar horsepower 1150. This run was completely clear of checks, and the train arrived at Kings Cross 3¼ min early instead of schedule. The net times on these four runs gave start-to-stop average speeds of 65.6, 67.3, 67.7 and 65.6 mph which would have been almost undreamed of, when the first Great Northern Railway 'Pacifics' took the road.

Excellent though the service was provided on this crack Leeds express, it was perhaps the acceleration of the Anglo-Scottish service—and particularly the 1.20 pm down from Kings Cross —that was principally gratifying. The load of the 1.20 was rarely less than 'fifteen', which though it included a triplet articulated dining car set, rarely scaled less than 480 tons tare. I have tabulated details of four runs on Scotch expresses between Kings Cross and Grantham,

A record-breaker of 1932: No 2744 *Grand Parade*

which between them show some outstanding work. The first, with a Gateshead engine and driver shows what we came to regard as a run-of-the-mill performance on the 1.20 pm, allowed 114 min to Grantham. There were no checks of any kind and *Trigo* took this 515-ton train steadily uphill, and swiftly down, to arrive in Grantham 1½ min early. On the second run *Neil Gow*, a Heaton engine, had the 10.5 am 'Junior Scotsman' on the summer service, and was following close on the heels of the 'non-stop'. This train then had the severe allowance of 111 min to Grantham, equal to that of the up Leeds 'Breakfast Flyer' until May 1932, but now expected to be maintained with a load of over 500 tons. Like all other engines in this table *Neil Gow* was working through to Newcastle. The correspondence in times between this engine and *Trigo* as far as Yaxley was remarkable. Then the very heavy traffic of a summer Saturday delayed *Neil Gow* in the Peterborough area, but there is no doubt that the difficult 111 min timing would have been kept, with a clear road.

It is next the turn of Kings Cross shed, and my first experience of the accelerated service,

LNER KINGS CROSS—GRANTHAM

Dist miles	Engine No ,, Name Load tons E/F	2595 *Trigo* 477/515 Actual m s	Speeds mph	2581 *Neil Gow* 491/525 Actual m s	Speeds mph	2744 *Grand Parade* 497/530 Actual m s	Speeds mph	2579 *Dick Turpin* 516/550 Actual m s	Speeds mph
0.0	KINGS CROSS	0 00	—	0 00	—	0 00	—	0 00	—
2.6	Finsbury Park	6 40	—	6 53	—	6 20	—	6 28	—
5.0	Wood Green	9 56	53½	10 08	53½	9 35	54½	9 55	53
								pws	10
9.2	New Barnet	15 25	42	15 22	46	14 47	45½	16 00	—
12.7	Potters Bar	20 25	42	20 15	42½	19 37	43½	22 57	36½
17.7	HATFIELD	25 30	72½	25 25	72	24 40	75½	28 19	72½
23.5	*Woolmer Green*	30 55	56	30 57	56	29 45	60	33 46	57
28.6	Stevenage	35 43	69/65	35 50	68/65	34 22	71/67	38 40	69/62
31.9	HITCHIN	38 27	80½	38 36	80½	37 00	82	41 38	78
			86½		86½		87½	pws	30
41.1	Biggleswade	45 13	—	45 23	—	43 35	—	51 58	75
51.7	St Neots	53 40	68	53 57	68½	51 55	69½	61 04	68
58.9	HUNTINGDON	59 33	75	59 56	75	57 37	78	67 05	75
63.5	Abbots Ripton	64 08	55½	64 29	56	61 58	59	71 40	55
69.1	Holme	68 53	79	69 18	77½	66 45	78	76 36	75½
76.4	PETERBOROUGH	76 55	—	sigs 77 15	—	73 55	—	83 42	—
79.5	*Werrington Jc*	82 22	53	sig stop 86 06	50	78 57	53	88 35	57/64½
								pws	25
88.6	Essendine	91 55	60	95 43	61½	89 00	57½	99 05	—
							38/46		50
100.1	*Stoke Box*	105 52	44½	sigs 109 30	—	104 37	40	114 00	44
				sigs					68
105.5	GRANTHAM	112 30	—	117 52	—	111 30	—	120 15	—
	Net times	112½		111½		111½		111¼	

on the 1.20 pm was the kind of thing one is never likely to forget. In the previous chapter examples were quoted of widely dissimilar ways of running between Kings Cross and Peterborough, with *Felstead* losing 5½ min to Hatfield and then clocking into Peterborough 3½ min early. On this run of mine *Grand Parade* made a splendid start, despite a wet rail and continuous rain, and then went on in the style of *Felstead*, but with an even heavier load. The result was that we were through Peterborough in the astonishing time of 73 min 55 sec—7 min early! With quite easy running up to Stoke we arrived at Grantham 2½ min early. The last of the four runs was on the *Flying Scotsman* itself, allowed 116 min to Grantham. This was a winter occasion, with three bad permanent way checks in operation, and driving rain and sleet all the way from Kings Cross to York. The train was worked by a Heaton engine and men, and although time was lost, it was a highly creditable performance. Note should be taken of the splendid start out of Kings Cross, with 550 tons; the very fast running from Biggleswade, without any of the usual impetus from a fast run down

from Stevenage, and the hard work on both sides of the Essendine check. The three slacks cost fully 9 min between them, leaving a net time of 111¼ min.

It was only on the last of these four journeys that we got a reasonably clear run through to York. If connections from the Eastern Counties to the North were running late it was the practice to stop the London trains at Doncaster to take up passengers, and this happened to both *Trigo* and *Neil Gow*. On the other hand *Grand Parade's* hurricane progress came to a premature end, at Newark, where she had to come off the train due to heating troubles. So far as power output was concerned, *Dick Turpin* would appear to have shown the highest performance, in the finely sustained effort from Biggleswade onwards. This involved an equivalent drawbar horsepower of just over 1000, at 69 mph and a drawbar pull of about 2½ tons. Nevertheless without knowledge of the actual engine working it is difficult to assess the effect of the wintry working weather conditions. The BR train resistance value of 10.4 lb per ton, at 69 mph increases to 12.2 lb per ton, if the train

The 1.20 pm Scotsman passing Harringay: engine No 2552 *Sansovino*

York–Edinburgh express near Darlington: engine No 2581 *Neil Gow*

is running against a 10 mph head wind blowing at 45° to the track. The drawbar horsepower to haul 550 tons at 69 mph on the level in such conditions would be around 1200.

Some interesting results of indicator trials with the 'A3' engine No 2751 *Humorist* were quoted in a paper read before the Institution of Locomotive Engineers in March 1947 by Mr Spencer, and the details are plotted on the accompanying diagram. The tests were taken with a train of 540 tons, and it will be seen that the maximum indicated horsepower of around 1700 was obtained when working in 35 per cent cut-off at 40 mph. The general curve of performance shows a maximum indicated horsepower of about 1600, at 50 mph tailing off to about 1400 at 80 mph. What is, however, still more interesting is to see how the three cylinders contribute to the total horsepower.

Speed mph	Cut-off %	Indicated Horse Power			
		LH	Middle	RH	Total
43	30	463	513	527	1503
57	25	460	553	518	1531
63½	20	384	547	472	1403
75	20	402	585	480	1437

It will be seen that the right hand outside cylinder was doing more work than the left hand throughout this range of speed and cut-off, and at 43 mph, within limits, the three cylinders were taking a fair share of the work. But as the speed increased, the inherent tendency of the inside piston valve to over-run became more and more pronounced until, at 75 mph, the middle cylinder was doing no less than 45 per cent more work than the left hand outside one, and 22 per cent more than the right hand one.

From this it will be appreciated that the cut-offs indicated on the scale, mounted in an ideal place for the observer to see on the boiler faceplate, could not be anything but nominal. It might give a fair indication of what was happening in the outside cylinders, but the inside one would obviously be working in a far longer cut-off. It may well be that the size of the driving crank pins had been proportioned with the view of compensating for these inequalities. The outside pins were 5½ in diameter by 6 in long, while the middle one was 8¼ in diameter and also 6 in long. Of course the middle 'crank pin' was also the mid-point of the built-up driving axle, and the strength of this would have been a determining factor, rather than the bearing surface provided for the drive from the middle cylinder. But, as I shall tell later, this increased bearing surface did not

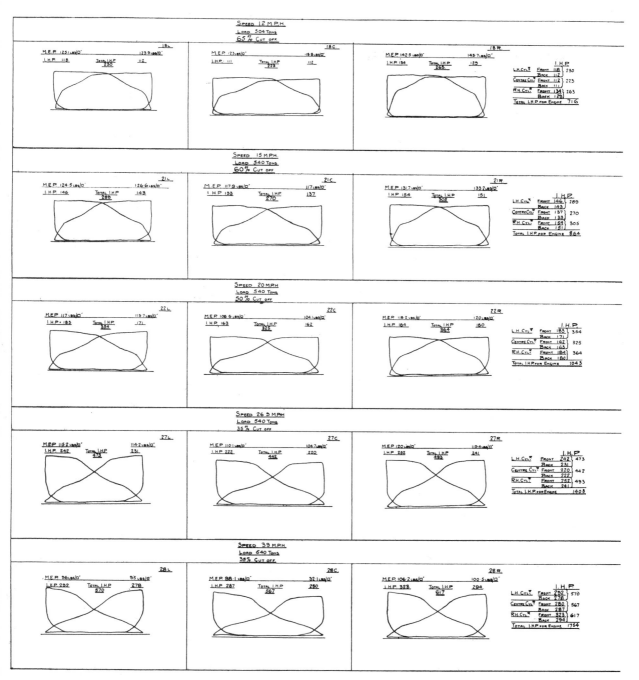

Indicator tests on No 2751 *Humorist*

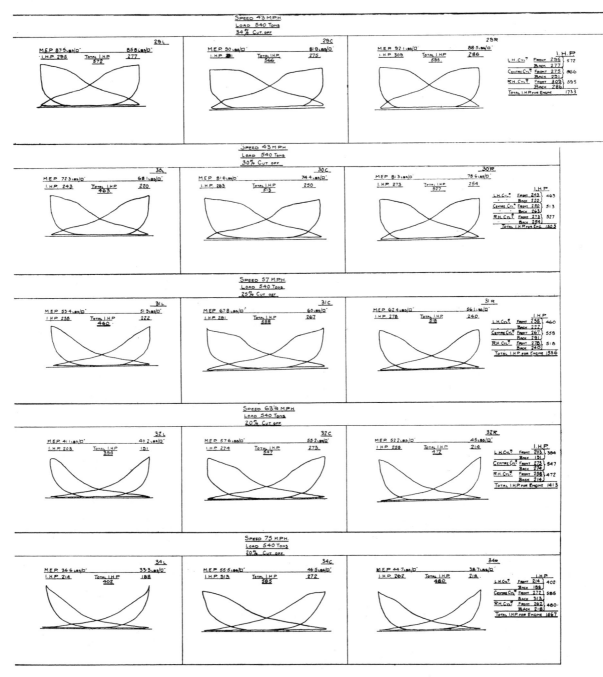

Indicator tests on No 2751 *Humorist*

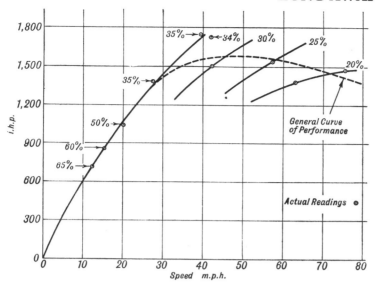

Horsepower diagram: engine No 2751 *Humorist*

prevent the occasional feailure of the middle big end.

Gresley always claimed that his 'Pacifics' had been designed for hauling 600-ton loads, and the accelerations of May 1932 put no restraint on the operating department to pile on the 'tons' when they so desired. The up 'Flying Scotsman' seemed a favourite train for 600-ton loading, and not only during the winter months. I was travelling from Edinburgh to Leeds one

The up 'Scarborough Flier' leaving Peascliff Tunnel, near Grantham: 'A3' class engine No. 4480 *Enterprise*

THE GRESLEY PACIFICS

day in 1932, and used the 'Junior Scotsman', as far as Darlington. With a 450-ton train No 2577 *Night Hawk* made an undistinguished run as far as Newcastle; but there the load was made up to 546 tons tare, 590 tons gross, and the London engine No 2561 *Minoru* came on. The stretch from Newcastle to Darlington, with its numerous permanent way hindrances, was a tiresome one in those days, and there was little chance for *Minoru* and her keen driver to show their paces; but runs with two of the London 'A3s', *Fairway* and *Papyrus* show what could be done when the loads well exceeded 600 tons.

Fairway was logged throughout from Newcastle, with an 18-coach train of 615 tons gross, and a mere 37 sec were dropped on the 48 min schedule then in operation to Darlington. This minute loss was regained on the next stage, by running the 44.1 miles to York in 45 min 13 sec against an allowance of 46 min. Then the 82.7 miles to Grantham took $93\frac{3}{4}$ min, a loss of $1\frac{3}{4}$ min, and there was a net loss of only 2 min on the 116 min schedule for the final 105.5 miles to Kings Cross. An interesting feature of this long, strenuous working was that an aggregate of 200 miles was covered at an average speed of 60 mph and that the total of the net running times for the 268.3 miles run add up to no more than 305 min, an average speed of 52.9 mph. The run of *Papyrus*, on the same train with an identical load came exactly a week later, in January 1933, but was logged from Grantham only. Summary details of these two 615-ton runs are shown in the accompanying table.

LNER GRANTHAM–KINGS CROSS 'The Flying Scotsman'					
Engine 'A3' No			2746		2750
,, Name			*Fairway*		*Papyrus*
Load, tons E/F			580/615		579/615
Dist miles		Sch min	Actual m s		Actual m s
0.0 GRANTHAM .	.	0	0 00		0 00
5.4 *Stoke Box* .	.		11 06		10 30
8.4 Corby . .	.		14 32		13 38
26.0 *Werrington Jc* .			29 05		—
			sigs		
29.1 PETERBOROUGH		33	34 43		31 34
42.0 Abbots Ripton .			51 36		46 23
46.6 HUNTINGDON .		53	57 00		51 26
73.6 HITCHIN . .		80	84 03		76 25
87.8 HATFIELD .		96	102 21		92 25
			sigs		
102.9 Finsbury Park .			117 15		106 47
					sigs
105.5 KINGS CROSS .		116	122 38		115 00
Net time			118		112

The second of these two runs must have included some magnificent running; but unfortunately no details of intermediate maximum and minimum speeds were taken. A fair idea of them may be gained from those that occurred on a run of my own in June of that year when we had a load of 565 tons and engine No 4472 *Flying Scotsman*. From Peterborough the time on to Huntingdon was 40 sec faster; to Hitchin 33 sec slower; to Hatfield 23 sec faster, and to Finsbury Park 11 sec faster. So that over the

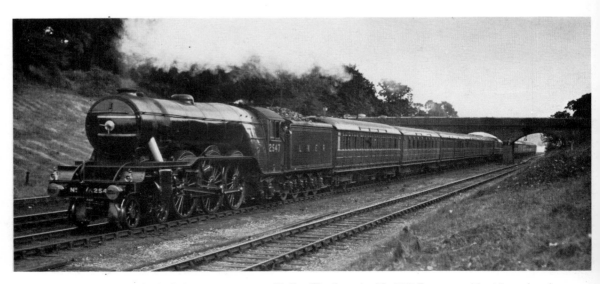

5.30 pm Newcastle dining car express near Hadley Wood: engine No 2547 *Doncaster* with a 15-coach train

73.8 miles from Peterborough to Finsbury Park *Flying Scotsman*, with 565 tons took 74 min 33 sec, and *Papyrus* with 615 tons took 75 min 13 sec—very level pegging indeed. Before taking the discussion of working these very heavy trains on to the almost level stretch of line between York and Darlington, there is one more Brobdingnagian effort to be mentioned, south of Peterborough, when another 'A3', No 2744 *Grand Parade* had to tackle a 19-coach train weighing 660 tons behind the tender. A Grantham 'A1', No. 2549 *Persimmon* had gained nearly 6 min on schedule from Doncaster, by running the 79.4 miles to Peterborough in $85\frac{1}{4}$ min. Then *Grand Parade* came on, and made a rather leisurely start, not reaching more than 57 mph across the Fens, and falling to $36\frac{1}{2}$ mph up Abbots Ripton bank. But having lost $1\frac{3}{4}$ min to Huntingdon the continuation was superb. The ensuing 56.3 miles to Finsbury Park took 56 min 28 sec, only a minute more than *Papyrus* with her 615-ton load on the 'Flying Scotsman'.

It is important in making an appraisal of these heavy load workings to examine the approximate power outputs involved. The stretch from Yaxley to Arlesey makes a good ground for examination. The speeds are roughly the same at the commencement and end of the length, and the gradient is adverse only to the extent of 1 in 2200. Over this section of 35.6 miles *Fairway* averaged 57.7 mph; *Grand Parade* 56.3 mph; *Flying Scotsman* 62.5 mph

and *Papyrus* 61.5 mph. As a consensus of performance one could take, therefore, an average of 60–61 mph with a 615-ton train. Taking a train resistance figure of 9.5 lb per ton, to allow for winter working conditions the equivalent drawbar horsepower works out at a little under 1100. Comparing this with the figures of *indicated* horsepower obtained from the 'A3' engine *Humorist* rather suggests that the engines with the 600-ton trains were being worked little harder than normal, with cut-offs of 20 to 22 per cent and a wide open regulator.

The Darlington–York section provides an extremely interesting test ground for observing high speed performance, and here I have tabulated details of five runs with loads ranging from 440 up to 620 tons. Between Otterington and Beningbrough, both passed at high speed, the average descending gradient is 1 in 2230—seemingly little removed from dead level, and the analysis of these five runs gives the following results.

Engine No	Load tons	Av speed mph	DHP Calculation train resistance	Correction for gradient	EDHP
2597	440	78	1093	−125	968
2750	495	72	1020	−125	895
4475	515	75.8	1178	−136	1042
4472	565	$72\frac{1}{2}$	1165	−140	1025
2746	620	$69\frac{3}{4}$	1200	−145	1055

On the first run of the four the Gateshead engine No 2597 *Gainsborough* was running at a steady 82–83 mph on dead level track between Thirsk

LNER DARLINGTON—YORK

Engine No „ Name Load, tons E/F					2597 Gainsborough 417/440	2750 Papyrus 469/495	4475 Flying Fox 471/515	4472 Flying Scotsman 528/565	2746 Fairway 579/620
Dist miles					Actual m s	Actual m s	Actual m s	Actual m s	Actual m s
0.0 DARLINGTON	.	.	.		0 00	0 00	0 00	0 00	0 00
2.6 Croft Spa	.	.	.		4 28	4 36	5 03	4 57	5 13
5.2 *Eryholme Jc*	.	.	.		7 13	7 28	8 01	7 56	8 18
14.1 NORTHALLERTON	.	.			14 56	15 39	16 20	16 29	16 55
17.5 Otterington	.				17 39	18 35	19 20	19 29	19 55
21.9 THIRSK	.				20 51	22 13	22 53	23 02	23 31
28.0 Pilmoor	.				25 18	27 30	27 52	28 10	28 50
32.9 Alne	.				29 09	31 42	31 44	32 13	33 00
38.6 Beningbrough	.	.			33 53	36 11	36 18	36 54	38 05
					—	—	—	sig stop	—
42.5 *Poppleton Jc*	.	.			37 36	39 32	39 45	41 28	41 50
—					sigs	—	sig stop	—	sigs
44.1 YORK	.	.			41 08	42 43	45 05	47 00	45 13
Maximum speed mph					$83\frac{1}{4}$	74	$77\frac{1}{2}$	75	$72\frac{1}{2}$
Av speed, Otterington to Beningbrough mph					78	72	$75\frac{3}{4}$	$72\frac{1}{2}$	$69\frac{3}{4}$

and Pilmoor, and unless she was being helped by a following wind, this was the highest power output of all, 1250 dhp. The published log states that the engine was eased after passing Pilmoor. This was probably because they were getting ahead of time, and not because the high power output was 'beating the boiler'.

The effect of the slight adverse gradient is noticeable in the difference normally to be observed on northbound trains. At the same time one must make allowance for conditions likely to prevail on the footplate at that stage of a through London–Newcastle working. While on the southbound run an engine would be nicely warmed up by the time Darlington was left, and in 'cracking' form, a Kings Cross fireman going north once explained to me that York to Darlington was usually their roughest patch. Between Beningbrough and Northallerton the rise averages 1 in 1630, and the horsepower results from two good runs of my own were thus:

Engine No	Load tons	Av speed mph	DHP Calculation		EDHP
			Train resistance	Correction for gradient	
2595	515	61.8	815	150	965
4476	520	63.4	855	157	1012

Both engines were working through from London, and with 4476 *Royal Lancer* I was on the footplate. The engine was being worked in 25 per cent cut-off throughout, with the regulator not fully opened, and steam chest pressure about 140 lb per sq in.

From these different observations in a considerable variety of conditions it would seem that the general standard of performance of the 'A1' and 'A3' was to provide equivalent drawbar horsepower outputs of 1000 to 1100. So far as driving techniques were concerned, most enginemen seemed to use wide-open regulator, and cut-offs of 20 per cent or less whenever possible on the 'A3s'. On the 'A1s' some of the drivers preferred to use regulator openings something less than full, and cut-offs of 20 to 25 per cent. The engines of both series were most comfortable and enjoyable to ride, and there was an almost total lack of vibration, either from the suspension or the motion. Things were made doubly interesting for the observer by the fitting of steam chest pressure gauges, which are always so useful for assessment of the working when a driver is using less than a full regulator opening. On the 'A1s' there was usually a drop of about

15 lb per sq in between boiler and steam chest, when full regulator was being used—175 to 160 lb per sq in was a typical figure. On the 'A3s' the difference was generally a little less, about 10 lb per sq in.

Generally speaking the 'Pacifics' of both 'A1' and 'A3' classes attained a very high degree of reliability, though this chronicle of the history of both classes must include a reference to that one point of weakness in the design that did let them down badly, on occasions—the middle big-end. It so happens however that at certain times when this occurred, and there were critical observers on the scene, the rescue operations were so swift and spectacular as to

The 'Scarborough Flier' leaving Kings Cross: engine No 4473 *Solario*

erase any sense of stigma, and have the observer feeling that he could not be sorry the *contretemps* had taken place! At this point I might mention the arrangements that existed on the East Coast Route, of having 'standing pilots' at many major running sheds en route. It was noticed particularly when the 'non-stop' 'Scotsman' was first introduced. The normal practice was to have 'Pacifics' available on the down side at Grantham, Doncaster, York and Newcastle, with 'Atlantics' standing pilot at Hitchin, Peterborough, Darlington and Tweedmouth. On the up side there were 'Pacifics' at Newcastle, Doncaster and Grantham, and 'Atlantics' at the other five sheds. In the North Eastern Area two 'Atlantics' stood all day, one at each end of the station at Darlington, and also at Tweedmouth shed.

The most widely-known failures all occurred on the 1.20 pm down 'Scotsman', and two of these were with the same engine, No 2744 *Grand Parade*. The first took place on the day of the very fast run to Peterborough (see page 114). We had started away from Grantham, but before Newark the driver scented trouble, and slowing down short of the station he stopped abreast of an 'Atlantic' that was on a slow train in a siding. On the second, third and fourth occasions the 'Pacific' was left at Grantham, and in each case the substitute 'Atlantic' covered itself with glory. I noted two other occasions where 'Pacifics' were in trouble. On the 2.5 pm up from Waverley on which a Gateshead engine normally worked through to York, No 2569 *Gladiateur* was steaming poorly with a 475-ton train. She took 76 min 52 sec to pass Berwick and then stopped at Tweedmouth to take the pilot. Information was sent on ahead for Newcastle to have a fresh engine ready, because No 2569 was in no state to continue through to York. At Tweedmouth a North Eastern 'Z' class 3-cylinder 'Atlantic' was coupled on ahead, and the two engines together made a fast run to Newcastle. Two fresh 'Atlantics' then took

over, and it was only at York that the normal working of the train was resumed. To the credit of all concerned the whole of the lost time was recovered, and we were running on time soon after Doncaster.

On the down 'Flying Scotsman', just before the Whitsun holiday one of the Heaton engines, No 2579 *Dick Turpin* with a 16-coach train of 545 tons, was steaming very badly, and having taken $93\frac{1}{2}$ min to reach Peterborough stopped there to take the down pilot, 'Atlantic' No 4407. Leaving 20 min late the two engines made some fast running, and would have recovered about 8 min to York; but a prolonged signal stop outside for 9 min, threw it all away. Furthermore, on this very busy day there was no spare engine, or men available to give assistance north of York. The luckless men on No 2579 were told to do the best they could, with the result that a good deal more time was lost to Newcastle. There the fresh engine, oddly enough, was a London 'A3', No 2746 *Fairway*, but the crew did no more than keep point-to-point time, and with signal checks we were nearly 40 min late into Edinburgh. I have perhaps given a certain degree of prominence to these less glorious exploits; but during the 1930s there was a tendency to extoll the Gresley 'Pacifics' to a

5.30 pm Newcastle dining car express on Ganwick Curve: engine No 2561 *Minoru*

degree a little out of proportion to their true status, and it is only fair in a chronicle of this kind to give both sides of the picture.

In four years from the introduction of the accelerated timings of 1932 I made forty runs with Gresley 'Pacifics' and on five of these there was either complete failure, as with No 2744 at Newark, the provision of pilot assistance, or appreciable loss of time due to shortage of steam. This is no place to make comparisons with the records of other classes of locomotives; but I am bound to say that in a period when reliability of British locomotives was at a notably high level, the occasion in my own travelling experience when the Gresley 'Pacifics'

were in trouble seemed disproportionately high. I may have been unlucky, but this experience must be set on record. The graph of their technical performance as exemplified by the indicated horsepower readings taken from Engine No 2751 *Humorist*, on page 119, confirms their consistent ability to haul one of the 'standard' 15-coach East Coast trains including a triplet articulated dining car set—520 gross tons—at about 70–72 mph on level track. The maximum I noted personally in pre-war years was a sustained speed on the level of 74 mph, southbound between Selby and Doncaster, with a load of 540 tons, a drawbar pull of 2.7 tons, and a horsepower of 1200.

Aberdeen–Kings Cross express at York: engine No 2559 *The Tetrarch*

CHAPTER 9

HIGH SPEED TRIALS : 1934–5

When writing of the Gresley 'Pacifics', no matter how much discussion there may be about boilers, valve gears, suspension and such like, one comes inexorably back to the matter of high speed—really high speed; for it was in the attainment of speeds of 100 mph and over that these engines not only 'hit the headlines' but began a movement very far removed from mere showmanship. It was hard commerce, the full implications of which we are only now seeing developed on the nationalised British Railways. As to the situation in the early 1930s I cannot do better than quote from Sir Nigel Gresley's Presidential Address to the Institution of Mechanical Engineers in October 1936:

In 1932 a new stage in the development of railway operation was initiated by the introduction of extra high-speed railcar services. Railways on the Continent, particularly in Germany, and in the U.S.A., were being badly hit by the competition from road and air services. The facilities for rapid transit afforded by air services were proving very attractive. The diesel engine had reached a high state of development and railway engineers in conjunction with the diesel engine manufacturers produced diesel-electric railcars capable of maintaining much higher average speeds than those of the steam train.

The fast railcar afforded many obvious advantages over the road competition. It could run at higher average speeds over the well-laid railway tracks effectively controlled by an efficient system of signalling, and consequently with much greater safety. It also afforded many advantages over air transport because of its safety and reliability and independence of weather conditions. Incidentally the costs of transportation were cheaper. Furthermore, what it lost in speed as compared with air services it gained in being able to pick up and set

down its passengers at railway stations situated in the heart of the great cities instead of at an aerodrome located some miles away. In many cases journeys by road to and from the aerodromes had to be made through congested areas and consequently much of the advantage of the high average flying speed was lost.

In a different scale of speed Gresley might well have been speaking of the conditions of today, rather than those of nearly forty years ago! He then went on to tell how the *Flying Hamburger* was put into regular service in May 1933, and that its average speed between Berlin and Hamburg was 77.4 mph. He continued:

I visited Germany in the latter part of 1934 and travelled on the *Flying Hamburger* from Berlin to Hamburg and back; I was so much impressed with the smooth running of this train at a speed of 100 mph which was maintained for long distances, that I thought it advisable to explore the possibilities of extra high-speed travel by having such a train for experimental purposes on the London and North Eastern Railway.

I accordingly approached the makers of that train, and furnished them with full particulars as to the gradients, curves, and speed restrictions over the line between Kings Cross and Newcastle . . .

But Gresley was at heart a steam man, and earlier in this same address he had said:

The steam locomotive has always had a fascination for engineers, which is shared by many of the general non-technical public. One has yet to learn why the great electric or diesel locomotives seem to fail to command the interest produced by the steam engine. Viewed from the station platform, at the head of a long train, the steam locomotive, with its coupling and connecting rods exposed, is

125

alive and seems anxious to set off. Electric and diesel locomotives appear inert. It is much the same in an engine room of a great ship. No one will deny that the old fashioned reciprocating engines are far more fascinating than the modern steam turbine.

These were indeed moving words, from a President of the Institution of Mechanical Engineers in the year of Grace 1936, and going back to the autumn of 1934, it was not really surprising that while the Germans were working out their proposals for a *Flying Novocastrian* Gresley decided to have preliminary 'go' with steam. The *Flying Hamburger* carried 140 passengers, and so, at the end of November 1934, a test was arranged from Kings Cross to Leeds and back, and on the outward journey only four coaches were conveyed. On the test run, the dynamometer car was included; but for the tare weight involved, 145 tons, there would have been no difficulty in providing seating for 140 passengers. A schedule of $2\frac{3}{4}$ hr had been laid down in each direction, for the journey of 185.8 miles—an average speed of 67.6 mph; but careful arrangements were made throughout the route to keep the road clear well in advance of the prepared path, and the intention was to go as hard as possible to see how much time was in hand. In the conditions foreseen, much depended upon the temperament of the driver, and at that time one man particularly commended himself. W. Sparshatt had been making a name for himself on the Pullman trains, with 'Atlantic' engines, and he had recently been promoted to the Newcastle link, and allocated

to engine No 4472 *Flying Scotsman*. He was a hard runner, and, above all, a showman, and a natural choice for the high-speed Leeds trial. The point that raised doubts was the engine itself. She was never one of the best of the London 'Pacifics'; the running staff would have preferred 4474 or 4475 among the 'A1s', or better still, an 'A3'. But the trial was essentially one of feasibility, rather than of record breaking, and having an average rather than a superb engine could be an advantage.

There was however another factor that intruded. Gresley was intensely proud of his association with the LNER and held thinly-disguised ambitions to earn for it a position of undoubted pre-eminence in locomotive speed and performance. The return run from Leeds gave an opportunity to try for a record maximum speed down Stoke Bank, and Driver Sharshatt was undoubtedly the man to try for this. He would need little encouragement once the idea was mooted. It was in this, principally, that doubts were expressed about the particular engine. On the outward journey all the problems associated with the Anglo-Scottish 'non-stop' were prevalent, such as continuous steaming, lubrication, fatigue of the fireman, and such like. A load of no more than 147 tons behind the tender was not likely to tax the tractive capacity of the locomotive. Leaving Kings Cross at 9.8 am on Friday 30 November 1934 a fast and undelayed run was made throughout to Leeds, and on the special schedule the train was $3\frac{1}{2}$ min ahead by Huntingdon, $8\frac{1}{4}$ at Grantham, $10\frac{1}{2}$ min at Doncaster, and finally, 13 min

A London 'A1': No 4475 *Flying Fox*

Engine No 4472 *Flying Scotsman* at Kings Cross shed: Driver Sparshatt standing below the name plate

on arrival at Leeds. The principal passing times were as shown below.

Dist miles					Actual m	s	Speeds mph
0.0	Kings Cross .	.	.	.	0	00	—
12.7	Potters Bar .	.	.	.	13	16	57.5
17.7	Hatfield	.	.	.	17	03	79.2
31.9	Hitchin	.	.	.	28	22	75.2
58.9	Huntingdon .	.	.	.	46	31	89.3
76.4	Peterborough	.	.	.	60	39	74.3
100.1	Stoke Box .	.	.	.	79	33	75.3
105.5	Grantham	.	.	.	83	39	79.0
120.1	Newark	.	.	.	94	38	79.7
138.6	Retford	.	.	.	108	44	78.7
156.0	Doncaster	.	.	.	122	27	76.2
175.9	Wakefield	.	.	.	139	28	70.3
180.2	Ardsley	.	.	.	144	39	49.7
186.8	Leeds .	.	.	.	151	56	46.1

So far as the actual running was concerned, the outstanding items were the average speed of 90.2 mph over the 24.1 miles from Hitchin to Offord, with a maximum of $94\frac{3}{4}$ mph, and the ascent from Peterborough to Stoke summit. Here the average speed over the 18.2 miles from Helpston box to Stoke was 82.2 mph with a minimum of $81\frac{1}{4}$ mph. The average gradient is 1 in 314, and taking modern figures for train resistance the equivalent drawbar horsepower works out at no more than 875. On the upper part of the ascent however a speed of 82 mph

was sustained on 1 in 200, and this represents an output of 1145 edhp. The engine was however working in as much as 40 per cent cut-off, which was extremely high at such a speed as 82 mph. Tests with the 'A3' engine *Humorist* referred to on page 116 suggest that an engine of this latter class could develop 1500 *indicated* horsepower at 80 mph, or a little over, on no more than 20 per cent. Gresley himself quoted the horsepower needed to overcome the internal resistance of the engine, and the head-on air resistance at 80 mph as 450 horsepower with an 'A3' Pacific. This, in the case of *Humorist* would leave 1050 horsepower for traction, which would be enough to haul a 400-ton train at 80 mph on the level, or to take exactly the load of the Leeds test train, 145 tons, up a 1 in 200 gradient at 80 mph—but, on 20 per cent cut-off, not 40 per cent!

Apart from this somewhat inexplicable item the down test run was a 'romp'. One can quite imagine the operating authorities looking rather askance at a four-coach train, in view of what the 'Pacifics' were in the habit of hauling around, and for the return run two more coaches were added, making a gross trailing load of 207 tons. The engine and crew were evidently none the worse for the strenuous effort on the down journey, for despite the extra load time gaining

THE GRESLEY PACIFICS

began at once, and continued steadily until Grantham was passed, already $3\frac{3}{4}$ min early. Down the Stoke bank the driver had been advised beforehand that he could attempt a maximum speed record. The chart taken in the dynamometer car showed a maximum of exactly 100 mph, but it leaves doubts in one's mind, particularly as so experienced a recorder as the late Cecil J. Allen did not claim, from his own figures a higher speed than 98 mph. The graph is reproduced herewith, and it will be seen that while the rate of acceleration was quite uniform down the 1 in 200 approaching Little Bytham in the last mile it suddenly and substantially opened out, and eased again immediately afterwards. It is difficult to explain the shape of the speed curve about the 91st milepost. Be that as it may, the LNER officially claimed a maximum speed of 100 mph.

Passing Peterborough 8 min early the effort was considerably relaxed, and no further time was gained on the special schedule. The times are summarised in the adjoining log.

British railway history was surely made on that November day, when the weather was fortunately calm, and misty only in patches north of Doncaster. The entire round trip was made at an average speed of 72.2 mph, but it was

Dist miles		Actual m s	Av speed mph
0.0	Leeds	0 00	—
9.9	Wakefield	12 42	46.7
29.8	Doncaster . . .	30 58	65.4
47.2	Retford . . .	44 28	77.4
65.7	Newark . . .	58 28	79.3
80.3	Grantham . . .	70 18	73.7
85.7	*Stoke Box* . . .	74 54	70.5
106.3	*Werrington Jc* . .	89 00	87.7
109.4	Peterborough . . .	92 00	62.0
126.9	Huntingdon . . .	106 42	71.5
—		pw check	
153.9	Hitchin . . .	129 50	69.6
168.1	Hatfield . . .	141 11	75.0
183.2	Finsbury Park . .	153 22	74.5
185.8	Kings Cross . . .	157 17	

achieved on a somewhat inordinate consumption of coal. It was reported that a total of 9 tons of coal had been fired while on the run, an average of 54 lb per train mile. It was certainly a tribute to the stamina of Fireman Webster that he was able to sustain such an effort, which worked out at no less than 4000 lb per hour. This is 33 per cent greater than the maximum considered possible for a single fireman to maintain for any length of time, in the later days of British Railways—I know of only one other occasion when this rate of 4000 lb per hour was exceeded on a long run, and then the fireman had the assistance

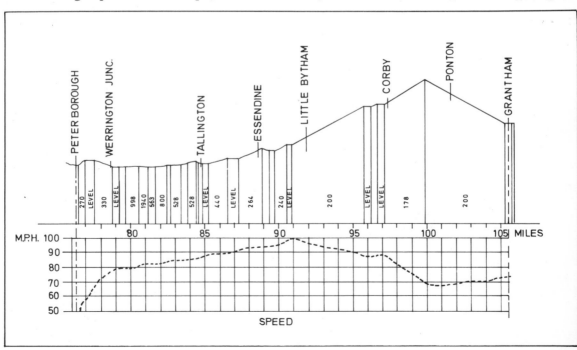

The 1934 London–Leeds records: chart of the up journey between Grantham and Peterborough

128

of a locomotive inspector, who helped him greatly by getting coal forward. This rather suggests that engine No 4472, while a 'big name' publicity-wise, was not altogether a happy choice for the job.

In the meantime the Germans had been getting busy working out possible schedules for a diesel-electric railcar train, similar to the *Flying Hamburger*, to run between Kings Cross and Newcastle. It was to consist of three articulated coaches, weighing 115 tons tare, and to carry, as in the German case, 140 passengers. But to everyone's surprise the best times that the Germans could offer were 4 hr 17 min southbound, and 4 hr $15\frac{1}{2}$ min northbound. The train that was maintaining an average speed of 77.8 mph between Berlin and Hamburg was expected to do no better than $62\frac{1}{2}$ mph between Kings Cross and Newcastle, such were the effects of the various speed restrictions encountered on the LNER. When it was also emphasised that the third class accommodation would be much more cramped than that regularly enjoyed by British passengers it was generally agreed that a railcar set of the *Flying Hamburger* type was definitely not on! It was then that Sir Ralph Wedgwood, Chief General Manager of the LNER suggested that far better times might be made with a six or seven coach train of standard coaching stock, and an ordinary steam 'Pacific' engine. So there was arranged the epoch-marking round trip from Kings Cross

to Newcastle and back, on 5 March 1935.

It was decided to use the same engine throughout, but obviously a round trip of 536.6 miles was too much for one crew, in a single day. This time one of the London 'A3s' No 2750 *Papyrus* was chosen, an engine with an excellent reputation. Since completion at Doncaster, in 1928, it had run 392,853 miles. It left Doncaster after a general repair in January 1935 and up to 4 March had run 7719 miles. It was just nicely run in. Both runs on 5 March were scheduled in the level 4 hr, and for the down journey the regular crew on No 2750, Driver H. Gutteridge and Fireman Wightman, were working, while for the return, the fire-eating Sparshatt and Fireman Webster were on.

The down journey was a remarkable performance. It was in many ways a complete epitome of the working characteristics of the 'A3' class at their normal best. Apart from short periods in accelerating from intermediate slacks, the only time when the engine was steamed really hard was in the ascent from Peterborough to Stoke summit. The average speed from Helpston box to Stoke was 76.6 mph on a gradient averaging 1 in 314. The equivalent drawbar horsepower sustained for about a quarter of an hour was 1050, while on the 1 in 200 approaching Corby the speed was held at 75 mph. Here the effort had been stepped up to 1325 edhp, and the indicated horsepower would have been about 1800. On the basis of the tests with

The up 'Flying Scotsman' leaving the Royal Border Bridge, Berwick: engine No 2571 *Sunstar*

THE GRESLEY PACIFICS

Humorist this would have required working in about 25 per cent cut-off. The train passed Grantham $4\frac{1}{4}$ min early in 87 min 42 sec from Kings Cross, and then an interesting hazard was thrown in the path of timekeeping, by a totally unexpected delay north of Doncaster on account of a freight train derailment. This cost fully 7 min in running, and the train was 4 min late in passing into the North Eastern Area at Shaftholme Junction.

The work by which this arrears was converted into an arrival in Newcastle 3 min early was some of the most interesting in the round trip. The tractive power of the locomotive, applied to no greater load than 217 tons, produced very rapid accelerations, from the emergency stop north of Doncaster, from Selby (passed at the prescribed reduced speed of 38 mph) and from York. Maximum speeds well in excess of 80 mph were attained following each of these accelerations, and the steady speed of 85 mph on the dead level at Thirsk involved an output of about 1150 drawbar horsepower. This was probably achieved with the reverser notched no further forward than 17 or 18 per cent. But perhaps the most remarkable feature of all in a run that yielded a net time of 230 min for the 268.3 miles from Kings Cross to Newcastle—70.2 mph average—was that the speed at no time exceeded 90 mph; in fact the absolute maximum was $88\frac{1}{2}$ mph. Without forcing the pace at any stage of the journey and with the most careful observance of all permanent speed restrictions, engine and crew had demonstrated that there was a full 10 min in hand on the 4-hr schedule.

In view of the attention presently being given to the further acceleration of the London–Newcastle service, with the proposed High Speed Diesel Train, and then the Advanced Passenger Train, it is interesting to bear in mind the locations where speed was required to be reduced, in 1935, and the speeds actually run thereat:

Offord	70	Ferryhill	65
Peterborough	20	Browney Colliery	45
Grantham	64	Durham	32
Retford	58	Lamesley	46
Selby	38	King Edward	
Chaloners Whin		Bridge Jc	24
Jc	52		
York	23		

On the return journey, after a turn-round time of 2 hr 40 min at Newcastle, the second engine crew was equally under instructions to attempt no more than point-to-point time-

LNER EXPERIMENTAL HIGH SPEED RUN
5 March 1935
Engine : 2750 *Papyrus* : Load : 217 tons

Dist miles		Actual m	s	Speeds mph
0.0	Kings Cross	0	00	—
17.7	Hatfield	18	03	58.8
31.9	Hitchin	29	19	75.7
58.9	Huntingdon	48	52	82.8
76.4	Peterborough	63	21	72.5
79.5	*Werrington Jc*	67	13	48.2
100.1		83	21	76.7
105.5	Grantham	87	42	74.5
120.1	Newark	99	10	76.5
138.6	Retford	115	18	68.8
156.0	Doncaster	132	00	62.5
—		sig stop		—
160.2	*Shaftholme Jc*	141	01	27.9
174.3	Selby	152	05	76.2
188.1	York	165	11	63.3
193.7	Beningbrough	170	36	62.0
210.3	Thirsk	182	50	81.3
218.1	Northallerton	188	34	81.5
232.3	Darlington	199	47	76.0
245.2	Ferryhill	211	06	68.5
254.2	Durham	221	07	54.0
267.7	*King Edward Bridge Jc*	235	10	57.7
268.3	Newcastle	237	07	—

Net time 230 min

keeping, with one exception, though the driver justifiably got a little time in hand in the early stages to offset a severe permanent way slowing over the site of the derailment, which had delayed the northbound run. The exception to close point-to-point running was to be between Grantham and Peterborough, where authority to attempt an exceptional maximum speed had been given. Some fine running was made on the faintly falling stretch between Northallerton and York, where the maximum of 88 mph was a close counterpart to the speed of 85 mph at Thirsk going north. By Shaftholme Junction 4 min was in hand; this proved adequate to offset the expected slowing over the accident site of the morning and Doncaster was passed on time. From this point to Grantham interest mounted in view of the evident nursing of the engine in readiness for a supreme attempt at a speed record down the Stoke bank.

It must be emphasised that this could be no ordinary piece of speeding. In the seven years since their first introduction the 'A3' engines had shown through numerous records of their running that their natural maximum down a 1 in 200 gradient was only a little over 90 mph. The experimental engine No 2544 *Lemberg*, with $18\frac{1}{4}$ in cylinders, had been logged at 93 mph, but she always appeared a little freer than the standard 'A3s'. If *Papyrus* was to attain a maximum of over 100 mph she was going to need 'pushing' a little, and steaming well over the normal rate of evaporation in the boiler. The fire needed preparation for this exceptional effort, and this is what the crew were doing particularly after Newark. Speed was allowed to fall to 59 mph on the 1 in 200 gradient past Barkston to Peascliff Tunnel, and nearly a minute was dropped on the 12 min allowance for the 14.6 miles from Newark to Grantham. It must have been difficult to avoid over-doing the building up process, for approaching Grantham there was a short spell of full 'blowing-off'! With Ross 'pop' safety valves there was always a marked drop in boiler pressure before they closed again, and approaching Grantham, instead of the full 220 lb per sq in which they had a minute or so earlier the pressure was only 190, with the steam chest pressure 170 and cut-off 22 per cent. It was an unfortunate start to the record attempt.

Passing Grantham the driver increased cut-off from 22 to 28 per cent, and during the climb to Stoke box, on a 1 in 198 gradient, the boiler was gradually rallied to 205 lb per sq in; but in this 5.4 miles speed gradually fell from $71\frac{1}{2}$ to $69\frac{1}{4}$ mph. The indicated horsepower was below

the standard of *Humorist* on the tests, being only about 1600. With maximum steam chest pressure one would have expected rather more than 1800 at a cut-off of 28 per cent; but instead of 200 or 205 lb per sq in in the steam chest *Papyrus* had only 178 to 185. Stoke Summit was passed at $69\frac{1}{4}$ mph, and the accompanying diagram, reproduced from a drawing made from the dynamometer car rcord, shows what happened subsequently. There is one reference on this 'official' diagram that admits of some doubt, and that is the note 'Regulator full open up to 85 mile post'. On the 'A3' engines, from many footplate experiences both before and after World War II I found that when the regulator *was* full open there was rarely more than 10, or at the most 15 lb per sq in pressure drop between the boiler and the steam chest. I had enough experiences, on many different engines of the class to discount any suggestion that inaccurate gauges contributed to this conclusion. However, before I enlarge upon the apparent discrepancies in the dynamometer car record we must note how the 1935 World Record speed with steam traction was set up.

For about 3 miles from Stoke summit the engine was worked in 22 per cent cut-off, and on a descending gradient of 1 in 178 speed

5.30 pm Newcastle express near Potters Bar hauled by 'A3' Pacific No 2750 *Papyrus*

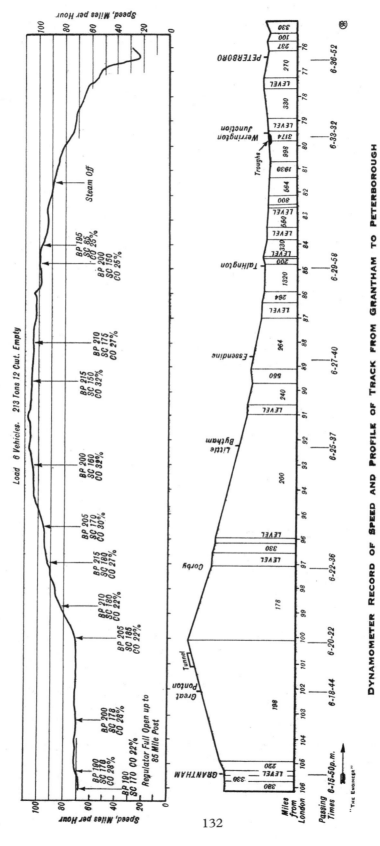

DYNAMOMETER RECORD OF SPEED AND PROFILE OF TRACK FROM GRANTHAM TO PETERBOROUGH

The great record of March 1935: speed chart of *Papyrus's* world record speed near Essendine

increased from $69\frac{1}{4}$ to 91 mph. The boiler pressure was now restored to 215 lb per sq in, and cut-off was increased to 27 per cent. Over the 'broken' descent between miles 97 and $95\frac{1}{2}$ this pushed up speed only to 95 mph, and a further increase was therefore made to 30 per cent cut-off, with steam chest pressure 170 lb per sq in. This, of course, was absolute 'thrashing' at such a speed, and as will be seen from the graph it took the speed fairly rapidly up to 104 mph whence it was sustained for about one mile. Then the driver tried a little more still, increasing cut-off to 32 per cent, and this produced the World Record maximum of 108 mph. It was magnificently sustained for some time afterwards, and in fact the 12.3 miles from Corby to Tallington were covered in no more than 7 min 20 sec—another world record for this distance of 100.6 mph. The engine was then justifiably eased, after having been steamed at about twice her normal rate for about 7 min.

Technically, a peculiarity of this spell of very heavy working was the variation in steam chest pressure. The following table merits close study.

Speed mph	Cut-off per cent	Boiler pressure psi	Steam chest pressure psi	Difference in pressure psi
80	22	210	180	30
90	27	215	180	35
95	30	205	170	35
104	32	200	160	40
108	32	215	150	65
104	27	210	175	35

It might be considered that at speeds in excess of 100 mph the cylinders were taking more steam than could get through the regulator and down the steam pipes to the steam chest, and that these pipes were proving a restriction and causing some lowering of the steam chest pressure. It will be seen that there was a gradual fall in this pressure from 90 mph irrespective of the boiler pressure, until the driver shortened his cut-off to 27 per cent just beyond Essendine station, and the steam chest pressure rose quickly to 175 lb per sq in. Admittedly there was a further sharp fall to 150 as the train approached Tallington, but it was then that the regulator was being eased a little also. All technicalities apart however, there were no half measures in the way the record was set up, and the engine suffered no ill after effects!

Neither apparently did the crew; for having passed Peterborough $5\frac{1}{4}$ min early they went on to make an exceptionally fast run up to

London, beating their previous record with 4472 in the previous November by a full 3 min. From Holme to Hatfield, against an average rising gradient of 1 in 1200 the speed averaged 80.5 mph representing a continuous output for nearly 40 min of 725 edhp and the indicated horsepower would have been about 1160. This suggests a reversion to normal maximum working of 15 to 17 per cent—again judging from the *Humorist* tests. The ultimate results created something of a sensation at the time, in the number and diversity of the world records set up; but a most important item was the coal consumption. The following figures were published afterwards by the LNER:

	Tons	Cwt
Coal issued at Kings Cross prior to down trip	9	5
Coal issued at Gateshead prior to return trip	5	0
Coal remaining when engine returned to Kings Cross	3	10
Total consumption, 536.6 mile round trip	10	15

This was equal to 45 lb per mile, a vast difference from the 54 lb per mile of the Leeds trip in the previous November. From the above figures one can make a guess, but only a guess at the relative consumptions on the down and up journeys on 5 March 1935. The corridor tenders had a coal capacity of 9 tons. If Gateshead were able to load 5 tons on it could be assumed that roughly 5 tons had been used on the down journey, equal to 42 lb per mile, leaving $5\frac{3}{4}$ tons for the up journey, that included the dash between Grantham and Peterborough and the preliminary stoking up that preceded it, 48.3 lb per mile.

The world records claimed for *Papyrus* were:
1. 12.3 miles at 100.6 mph
2. 500 miles (from Kings Cross to Croxdale and Croxdale back to Kings Cross) in 423 min 57 sec, or $412\frac{1}{2}$ min net, equivalent to 72.7 mph for 500 miles by one locomotive in one day with a 217-ton train.
3. 300 miles of one round trip at an average speed of 80 mph
4. The maximum speed of 108 mph

The summary logs of the two journeys are shown in the accompanying tables. For those who wish to study the runs in complete detail, very full reports were published in *The Engineer* 15 March 1935, and in *The Railway Magazine*

THE GRESLEY PACIFICS

for April 1935.

SOUTHBOUND EXPERIMENTAL RUN
5 March 1935

Dist miles					Actual m	s	Av speed mph
0.0	Newcastle .			.	0	00	—
14.1	Durham .			.	18	07	46.7
23.1	Ferryhill .			.	28	12	53.5
36.0	Darlington			.	38	53	72.5
50.2	Northallerton			.	49	15	81.4
58.0	Thirsk .			.	54	53	83.0
78.5	*Poppleton Jc*			.	69	40	83.3
80.1	York .			.	72	17	36.8
94.0	Selby .			.	86	38	58.2
108.1	*Shaftholme Jc*			.	99	03	68.2
—					pws		
112.3	Doncaster			.	106	40	33.1
129.7	Retford .			.	120	25	76.0
148.2	Newark .			.	135	52	71.8
162.8	Grantham .			.	148	42	68.3
168.2	*Stoke Box*			.	153	16	71.0
171.2	Corby .			.	155	28	80.2
183.5	Tallington			.	162	48	100.6
191.9	Peterborough			.	169	43	73.0
209.4	Huntingdon			.	185	00	68.7
236.4	Hitchin .			.	205	17	79.8
250.6	Hatfield .			.	216	23	76.8
265.7	Finsbury Park			.	227	58	78.3
268.3	Kings Cross			.	231	48	—

Net time 228 min

From the viewpoint of the future policy of the LNER the day's running was an immense success, and authority was given for design and construction to commence on the new high-speed train and locomotives, which emerged some five months later as the Silver Jubilee. Even before the trials of 5 March 1935 and indeed that of November 1934 had been run, a new batch of 'A3' Pacifics was in course of completion at Doncaster, and these included one new feature of design that had first been used on the 'P2' 2—8—2 engines, 'Cock o'the North' class. Instead of a simple dome, the boilers had a steam collector, in the form of a steel pressing, integral with the dome, as shown in the accompanying drawing. Steam was collected at a maximum height above water level both for the regulator and, from the rear end, for the steam valve manifold in the cab. There were nine of the new engines thus:

2500	*Windsor Lad*
2501	*Colombo*
2502	*Hyperion*
2503	*Firdaussi*
2504	*Sandwich*
2505	*Cameronian*
2506	*Salmon Trout*
2507	*Singapore*
2508	*Brown Jack*

They were mostly divided between Haymarket and Gateshead sheds, though No 2503 was at first shedded at Doncaster. While it cannot be

Down express on Langley troughs hauled by engine No 2550 *Blink Bonny*

First of the 1934 batch of 'A3s': No 2500 *Windsor Lad* with banjo dome

said that the 'banjo' steam collector, as it became known, improved the appearance of the engines, they settled down at once into excellent work. The Gateshead engines were frequently seen in London during the spring and summer of 1935 on the usual double-home turns, while No 2508 fitted with a corridor tender took a share in the working of the non-stop 'Flying Scotsman' during the summer season. In Scotland I rode on 2500 and 2506, the latter on the down Aberdonian in the early hours of the morning. It was an interesting occasion, as always when things go wrong! It was at a week-end in the very height of the summer, and the train was in two parts, and by some misunderstanding in the station working the engines waiting for the two sections were on the wrong side of Waverley station. With both going forward to Dundee it would not have mattered except that the second portion was apparently well over the Pacific load of 480 tons. An 'Atlantic' and a 'Scott' were waiting for it, but on the north side of the station! So *Salmon Trout* which was waiting on the far side of the station

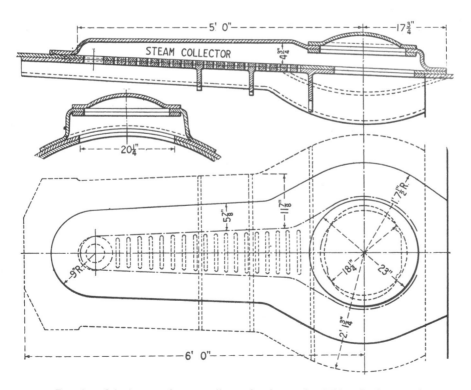

Drawing of the improved steam collector fitted to engine 2500 and subsequently

Up Newcastle express leaving Doncaster hauled by engine No 2503 *Firdaussi*

and this pair of ex-NBR engines had to be switched over.

But a far worse trouble developed when we started. The brakes were sticking on a coach somewhere down our long train, and until we could obtain release that 482 tons of train was pulling like 700 or 800 tons. The driver flailed the engine unmercifully. Memories of Sparshatt on *Flying Scotsman*!: this Haymarket man used full regulator and 57 per cent cut-off from Inver-

Edinburgh–Aberdeen express near Leuchars Junction: engine No 2506 *Salmon Trout*

One of the final batch of 'A3s', No 2504 *Sandwich*, at Kings Cross Top shed

keithing up to Dalgetty summit! Because of this we lost $10\frac{3}{4}$ min in the first 30 miles of the run, passing Thornton Junction, 30.7 miles in 54 min 43 sec. On releasing the brakes after observing the pitfall slack through that area, however, we got full release, and were able to continue to Dundee in grand style. Once we were over Lochmuir summit full regulator and

Aberdeen–Edinburgh express leaving Leuchars Junction: Class 'A3' engine No 2797 *Cicero*

THE GRESLEY PACIFICS

20 per cent cut-off enabled us to win back $2\frac{1}{2}$ min in the last 20.1 miles from Ladybank into Dundee, taking only $23\frac{1}{2}$ min for this stretch instead of the 26 min booked. But our total time over the 59.2 miles from Waverley was 90 min 35 sec. The keen Haymarket crew on No 2506 were as disappointed as I was with the overall loss of time, because the engine was in 'cracking' form.

With these references to the early work of the 2500–8 series of 'A3s' the story of the Gresley 'Pacifics' reaches its half-way stage. The saga of the 'A3s' was by no means ended, in 1935; in fact some of their finest work was done in the 1950s. But the introduction of the 'A4s' in the autumn of 1935, and their multiplication from 1937 made considerable changes in the working of the East Coast and Leeds services, and the second era can be conveniently left to the second volume.

Spreading their wings! One of a series of holiday resort postcards in which No 4472 was shown arriving at Paignton, Llandudno, and elsewhere! A 'train' was obviously a 'train' to the producers!!

HERBERT NIGEL GRESLEY

A BIOGRAPHICAL NOTE, TO MIDSUMMER 1935

Gresley, son of the Rev Nigel Gresley, Rector of Netherseale, near Burton-on-Trent, was born in June 1876, and educated at Marlborough College. He went to Crewe, LNWR, as an apprentice under F. W. Webb, and went subsequently to the LYR at Horwich, where he became a pupil of Sir John Aspinall. All his early experience following this training was on the Lancashire and Yorkshire Railway, and after appointments in the test department, and as running shed foreman at Blackpool he was, at the early age of twenty-five, made Assistant Works Manager at Newton Heath carriage works. In 1904 he became Assistant Superintendent of the Carriage and Wagon Department of the LYR. In 1905, when still under thirty years of age, he was appointed Carriage and Wagon Superintendent of the Great Northern

Railway, and in October 1911 he succeeded H. A. Ivatt as Locomotive Engineer. It is related elsewhere in this book how he was appointed Chief Mechanical Engineer of the LNER in February 1923. He was twice President of the Institution of Locomotive Engineers, in 1927–8, and in 1934–5, and when he became President of the Institution of Mechanical Engineers, in 1936, his Presidential Address was much concerned with the work described in the concluding chapter of this book. The subsequent volume, which will cover the later phases of the great 'Pacific' engine development, will refer to the many honours bestowed upon him subsequent to the year 1935. But one earlier distinction must now be mentioned; for it was in January 1920 that he was awarded the CBE for services during the first World War.

BIBLIOGRAPHY

Allen, Cecil J. 'British Locomotive Practice and Performance', *The Railway Magazine* (1922–35)

Gresley, H. N. 'The Three-Cylinder High-Pressure Locomotives', *Proc Inst Mechanical Engineers* (1925)

Nock, O. S. *Four Thousand Miles on the Footplate* (1952)

——. *LNER Steam* (1969)

——. *The Locomotives of Sir Nigel Gresley*

Presidential Address of Sir Nigel Gresley, *Proc Inst Mechanical Engineers* (1936)

ACKNOWLEDGEMENTS

The Author and Publishers wish to thank the following for permission to use photographs as follows:

Mrs Violet Godfrey, for pages 4, 10, 82

British Railways for pages 8, 11, 14, 15, 16, 21 top, middle and bottom, 42, 49 top, 53, 64 bottom, 65 top, 91, 116, 127, 135

M. W. Earley Esq, for pages 56 top, 107, 119, 120

R. B. Haddon Esq, for page 98

F. R. Hebron Esq, for page 66

K. H. Leech Esq, for pages 9, 17 top

Locomotive Publishing Co Ltd, for pages 17 bottom, 58

O. S. Nock Esq, for pages 37, 88, 129, 136 top, 137 top and bottom, 138

Real Photographs Ltd, for pages 5, 38, 39 top, 40, 41, 47, 48, 49 bottom, 51, 52 top, 52 bottom, 55, 56 bottom, 59, 60 top and bottom, 61, 62, 63, 64 top and bottom, 67, 70, 71, 72 top and bottom, 75, 76, 77, 79, 80, 84 top and bottom, 89, 90, 96, 97 top and bottom, 99, 101, 103 top and bottom, 104, 105 top and bottom, 106, 109, 114, 122, 123, 124, 126, 131, 134, 136 top

The late W. J. Reynolds, for pages 19, 39 bottom, 43, 46, 54, 59, 65 middle, 65 bottom, 68, 81, 85, 110, 115

E. R. Wethersett Esq, for pages 73, 83, 110, 112

The various drawings are published by courtesy of British Railways, and the indicator diagrams taken off engine No 2751 by courtesy of the Institution of Mechanical Engineers.

INDEX